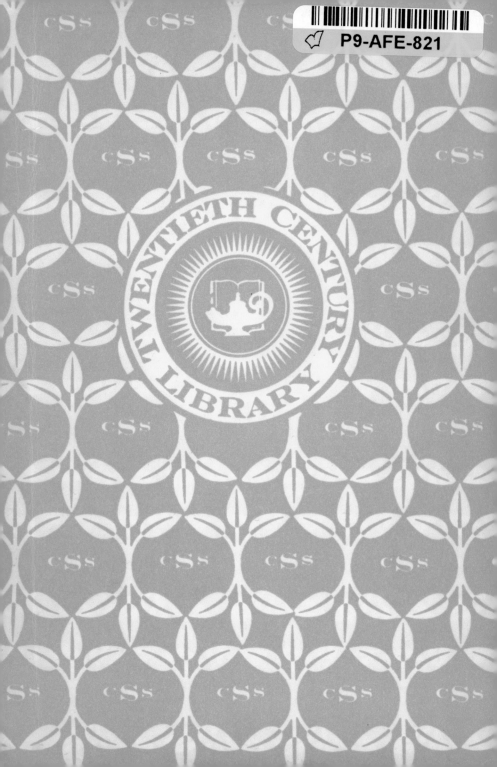

TWENTIETH CENTURY LIBRARY

Twentieth Century Library

Mahatma Gandhi

TWENTIETH CENTURY LIBRARY
    HIRAM HAYDN, EDITOR

Published:

MAHATMA GANDHI by Haridas T. Muzumdar
OSWALD SPENGLER by H. Stuart Hughes
SIGMUND FREUD by Gregory Zilboorg
JOHN DEWEY by Jerome Nathanson
JAMES JOYCE by W. Y. Tindall
CHARLES DARWIN by Paul B. Sears
ALBERT EINSTEIN by Leopold Infeld
GEORGE BERNARD SHAW by Edmund Fuller
FYODOR DOSTOEVSKY by Rene Fueloep-Miller
WILLIAM JAMES by Lloyd Morris

★

In Preparation:

KARL MARX by Max Lerner
FRANZ BOAS by Melville J. Herskovits
ALFRED NORTH WHITEHEAD by Stanley Newburger
HENRI POINCARÉ by Tobias Dantzig
THORSTEIN VEBLEN by David Riesman
JOHN MAYNARD KEYNES by Seymour Harris
FRIEDRICH NIETZSCHE by James Gutmann

CHARLES SCRIBNER'S SONS

HARIDAS T. MUZUMDAR

Mahatma Gandhi

PEACEFUL REVOLUTIONARY

CHARLES SCRIBNER'S SONS, NEW YORK

CHARLES SCRIBNER'S SONS, LTD., LONDON

1952

To

ALL THE CHILDREN OF AMERICA

this book is dedicated in the hope that their generation may capture something of the spirit of Mahatma Gandhi.

August 1, 1952

PREFACE

"THE LIGHT has gone out of our lives," said Prime Minister Jawaharlal Nehru, in an impromptu radio address upon Gandhi's martyrdom; "there is darkness everywhere." Could it really be that Gandhi's light ceased to shine since he was no longer with us in his puny bundle of flesh and bones? Correcting himself, Nehru continued: "I was wrong. For the light that shone in this country was no ordinary light. The light that has illumined this country for these many years will illumine this country for many more years; and a thousand years later, that light will be seen in this country, and the world will see it and it will give solace to innumerable hearts. For that light represented something more than the immediate present; it represented the living truth . . . the eternal truths, reminding us of the right path, drawing us from error, taking this ancient country to freedom." [1]

Gandhi may truly be said to be the prophetic voice of the twentieth century. Violence inflicts upon its practitioners physical and spiritual wounds; the way of non-violence, said Gandhi, "blesses him who uses it and him against whom it is used." [2] Again, "non-violence is the law of our species as violence is the law of the brute. The spirit lies dormant in the brute and he knows no law but that of physical might. The dignity of man requires obedience to a higher law—to the strength of the spirit." [3] Let us be sure we do not misunderstand the philosophy of non-violence embodied in Gandhi's life and teachings. A practitioner of the non-violent way of life, far from being passive, is the most active person in the world. He is ready to join the fray— non-violently—wherever and whenever there is injustice or wrong. He neither tolerates nor compromises with injustice, wrong, tyranny, authoritarianism, totalitarianism, dictatorship. His task in life is not to destroy the evildoer but to redeem and to convert the evildoer by love. "With malice toward none, with charity for all; with firmness in the right, as God gives us to see the right," he is ever ready to "bind up" humanity's "wounds," to minister to the underprivileged and to the misguided. The constant concern of the follower of non-violence is, in the words of Lincoln, to "achieve and cherish a just and lasting peace among ourselves and with all nations."

The spirit of India's Gandhi as well as of America's Lincoln is today sorely needed by a generation madly dancing over a precipice. We have learned to fathom the secrets of the atom, we have learned to master nature, but we have not yet learned to master our inner selves. Our scientists can predict with accuracy the long-range behavior and movements of stars and planets millions of miles away—but we are unable to foretell our next-door neighbor's behavior and movements the very next moment.

The world has become a small neighborhood. Therefore, we are called upon to understand and appreciate our neighbors across the Atlantic and the Pacific, as well as across the Great Lakes and the Gulf. To understand other nations, we must know their values and their historical development. This requires a sympathetic approach to other nations, cultures, and religions. By understanding Gandhi we may build a bridge of understanding between ourselves and India, between ourselves and the Orient, between ourselves and noble free spirits the world over.

What is Gandhi's message for our small neighborhood world divided into two camps—democratic and totalitarian? First of all, Gandhi would have us set our course by the twin stars of Truth and Non-Violence; which means, we must approach other peoples with charity and sympathy. Second, Gandhi would have us stand on a platform of values to which we must be faithful unto death; which means, we must act in accordance with principles, not expediency. Appeasement, even for the sake of peace, must be ruled out, because appeasement implies sacrifice of principles. Third, Gandhi would have us work ceaselessly for the realization of "common-human" values, as the sociologists say, for the triumph of the common-human way of life.

Gandhi did not believe in imposing his values or his way of life upon others; by the same token, he resisted even to death the attempts of others to impose upon him or his people their values and way of life. To be true to the Gandhi spirit, we may not, we cannot, think of *imposing* our democratic values and way of life upon the nations behind the iron curtain; nor would we permit those nations to impose their totalitarian values and way of life upon us. At the same time, the Gandhi way of life imposes upon us the obligation to *share* our democratic values and way of life with the peoples behind the iron curtain by open and non-violent methods.

According to Gandhi, there are three types of human beings: (1) the coward, (2) the brave, (3) the superior. The coward, in order to save his skin, supinely acquiesces in injustice and wrong. The brave hero, on the other hand, violently resists injustice and wrong in order to re-establish justice and right. The superior person is he who, in the fullness of his strength, forgives the wrongdoer and tries to redeem him and convert him to the ways of doing good.

As Americans we hold the first type—the despicable, cowardly type—in low esteem. Our choice today and tomorrow must be between the second and third alternatives. Let each one decide, in the light of his conscience, in terms of his definition of the situation, which alternative he must adopt in the present crisis.

Our generation is doomed to live in a state of perpetual crisis. You and I are called upon to be on the alert every moment of our lives. Truly, the price of liberty is eternal vigilance; but ceaseless effort and continuous vigilance, untempered by inner poise, are apt to lead to nervous prostration. Hence inner serenity in the midst of crisis must be cultivated if we are to safeguard our personal integrity, national freedom, and universal human values.

In Mahatma Gandhi we have a sure guide to a happy, rich, and meaningful life. A self-disciplinarian, he embodied the Hindu concept of the superior man—of the Mahatma, the Great Soul.

Any one of us can become a Mahatma if we make a vocation of
living the good life—putting principle above expediency, duty
above pleasure, service above profit, God above the world, conscience above fleeting rewards.

Throughout the text, except in quoted passages, the word
Hindese (derived from Hinda or Hind anglicized into India) has
been preferred to the word Indian in order to obviate confusion
between the Indians of India and the Indians of America.

The literature on Gandhi is growing apace. The very first
biographical sketch of Gandhi to appear in any language was a
work by Rev. Joseph J. Doke, entitled *M. K. Gandhi: An Indian
Patriot* (London: London Indian Chronicle, 1909). My book,
Gandhi the Apostle (Chicago: Universal, 1923), was the first
full-length portrait of the Mahatma to appear in any language of
the world. My second book, *Gandhi Versus the Empire* (New
York: Universal, 1932), was banned from India by the British
Raj. In *Gandhi Triumphant* (New York: Universal, 1939), I set
forth Mahatma Gandhi's philosophy of the fast and the story of
his victorious struggle with the Prince of Rajkot. *Sermon on the
Sea*, sometimes entitled *Indian Home Rule* or *Hind Swaraj*, written by Gandhi in South Africa in 1909, and edited by the present
writer in this country (Chicago: Universal, 1924), reveals
Gandhi's views on civilization and on soul force.

For a comprehensive biography the reader may refer to
The Life of Mahatma Gandhi by Louis Fischer (New York:
Harper and Brothers, 1950). For a commendable interpretation
of the mystic in Gandhi, read *Lead, Kindly Light* by Vincent
Sheean (New York: Random House, 1949). C. F. Andrews's
trilogy: *Mahatma Gandhi—His Own Story* (1930), *Mahatma
Gandhi's Ideas* (1930), *Gandhi at Work* (1931), all published by
The Macmillan Co., New York, are indispensable to an under-
standing of the man. *Nehru on Gandhi* (New York: The John
Day Co., 1948) is a splendid little book which everyone should
be familiar with. *Mahatma Gandhi: A Biography for Young
People* by Catherine Owens Peare (New York: Henry Holt and
Co., 1950) should be helpful especially to High School teachers

and pupils. The Navajivan Press, Ahmedabad, India, is getting
out a uniform series of topical books containing the Mahatma's
voluminous writings over the past forty years. The two volumes
containing Gandhi's writings in *Young India*, Ahmedabad, published in this country by B. W. Huebsch, Inc., New York, and by
The Viking Press, New York, respectively, as *Young India 1919–
1922* (1923), *and Young India 1924–1926* (1927), are a veritable gold mine for the researcher. Gandhi's autobiography: *My
Experiments with Truth*, recently published in full in this country
(Washington: Public Affairs Press, 1948), is a must reading.
Two books published in India have been particularly helpful to
me: *Gandhiji*, edited by D. G. Tendulkar and others (Bombay:
Karnatak Publishing House, 1944, 2nd ed., 1945), and *The Mind
of Mahatma Gandhi* by R. K. Prabhu and U. R. Rao (Madras:
Oxford University Press, 1945, 2nd ed., 1946). To Messrs. K. R.
Kripalani, Gulzarilal Nanda, and M. R. Masani I am indebted for
fresh material, respectively, on "Gandhi and Tagore," "A Charter
for Labor," and "Is Gandhi a Socialist?" appearing in *Gandhiji*.
Portions of my chapter on "Gandhi's Pedagogy" had appeared in
School and Society (Lancaster, Pa.), *Unity* (Chicago), and *The
Social Frontier* (New York). I am indebted to the authors and
publishers named, to Dr. Hiram Haydn, editor of this series, and
to countless others not named. Full credit is given in footnotes. So
far as possible, references, listed at the end, have been made to
books published in America. In addition to my three books on
Gandhi mentioned, I have drawn freely from my book, *The
United Nations of the World* (New York: Universal, 1942; 2nd
ed., 1944), especially for material embodied in Chapters III
and VII.

When all is said and done, my greatest debt is to the Saint
of Sabarmati, my association with whom at the Satyagraha Ashram, on the Dandi March, and in London, I count among the
greatest privileges in life.

HARIDAS T. MUZUMDAR

CORNELL COLLEGE
MT. VERNON, IOWA
MAY, 1952

CONTENTS

PREFACE   vii

CHAPTER   I.   *A CHILD OF ONE WORLD*   1

CHAPTER   II.   *THE MORAL EQUIVALENT OF WAR*   16

CHAPTER   III.   *SOUL FORCE—DESIGN FOR LIVING*   30

CHAPTER   IV.   *THE MAHATMA AND THE POET*   45

CHAPTER   V.   *GANDHI'S ECONOMICS*   57

CHAPTER   VI.   *GANDHI'S PEDAGOGY*   75

CHAPTER   VII.   *THE APOSTLE OF NON-VIOLENCE*   96

NOTES AND BIBLIOGRAPHY   115

CHRONOLOGY   121

INDEX   125

CHAPTER ONE

A CHILD OF ONE WORLD

1. THE UNIVERSAL IN GANDHI

MAHATMA GANDHI belongs not to India alone but to the whole world. He belongs not to our generation alone, not to the twentieth century alone, but to posterity as well. In life as in death Gandhi has been revered by millions of his compatriots in India and millions abroad. Most of us of the present generation look upon him as a great political leader. As such, Gandhi would no doubt be classified with the great makers and moulders of nations—Cromwell, Napoleon, Mazzini, Washington, and Lincoln. Future generations, however, will, I believe, recognize in Gandhi one of the greatest spiritual forces of all times.

Whether we knew much or little about him, this man in a loin-cloth somehow reminded the men of the present generation, and will continue to remind future generations, of the great heights which the spirit of man can scale. In him we see an image of our higher self, of that nobler self which recognizes non-violence and truth as the law of our species.

A proper understanding of Gandhi requires recognition of two strands woven in the makeup of his personality as of every human being: the universal and the particular.

Every human organism is subject to the universal biophysical processes of birth, growth, maturation, senescence, disintegration. Every human being, endowed with original nature, becomes human only as the original nature is transformed into human

1

nature through socialization, through social interaction within a cultural context. This, too, is a universal process in which all human beings become involved immediately upon birth. Mind, intelligence, intellect, emotion, insight, all rooted in the organism, come to flowering as a result of interaction with nature, with fellow human beings, with culture. In this process, the heart, a physiological organ, is spiritualized into a special instrument of insight; notice, for instance, Gandhi's frequent use of the idea: "Ultimately we are guided not so much by the intellect as by the heart." He made that statement upon our arrival at Dandi Beach, a forlorn, forsaken place, with few trees or habitations to relieve the monotony of the open, sun-baked landscape. In this process of interaction, too, the human potential, in contrast to the subhuman potential, becomes realized as the soul or spirit of man. Upon man's animal ancestry is superimposed a certain attribute, which distinguishes the world of human beings from the animal world. To the extent that man, by deliberate effort, achieves a way of living in which animal traits are subordinated to the distinctively human, to that extent does he realize his entelechy, his implicit destiny, a Greek concept—or his *dharma,* a Hindu concept. Such a way of living brings man near unto God. The realization of his soul, his self, becomes tantamount to realization of the Supreme Soul, the Supreme Self, or God.

This mode of reasoning, implicit in Hindu thinking, should not be unacceptable to social scientists. At any rate, Gandhi accepted the theory of the distinctively human traits differentiating man from the subhuman creation. "Non-violence," he affirmed, "is the law of our species as violence is the law of the brute. The spirit lies dormant in the brute and he knows no law but that of physical might. The dignity of man requires obedience to a higher law—to the strength of the spirit." [1]

The distinctively human, or rather common-human, nature of man is succinctly described by Hindu seers in the formula: *Tat-Twam-Asi*—That thou art. You are part of That, part of the Godhead. You have within you some of the divine attributes. Indeed, you have, as the Quakers say, *that* of God within you. Thus man is a complex of animal-human-divine attributes. In some the animal traits predominate, in others the human, and in others again the divine: in the language of the Bhagavad Gita, some men are dominated by the *Tamas* quality, some by the *Rajas* quality, and some by the *Sattva* quality.

Man, a specific person, as a complex of animal-human-divine attributes, may be best understood if from his behavior patterns we get a clue to the dominant and recessive qualities of his being. Gandhi belonged to the company of those in whom *Sattva* or the divine attribute is dominant and the other two attributes are recessive.

Gandhi made much of conscience. He used to quote with approval a verse from the Mahabharata:

> *The individual may be sacrificed for the sake of the family;*
> *The family may be sacrificed for the sake of the village;*
> *The village may be sacrificed for the sake of the province;*
> *The province may be sacrificed for the sake of the country;*
> *For the sake of conscience, however, sacrifice all.*

What is this thing called conscience? The unsophisticated Polish peasant defined conscience as one's own voice but somebody else's words. We may look upon conscience as a highly developed instrument in the inner recesses of man's heart, a subtle part of evolving human nature specializing in sensitive reactions to the world round about oneself. Conscience manifests itself in terms of sensitivity to sufferings and injustices, to right and wrong. Thus conscience is the internalized experience of the *mores* of a given society. Non-totalitarian societies exalt freedom of conscience alike for atheists and for theists; for non-conformists as well as conformists; for Catholics, Protestants, and Jews; for Hindus, Muslims, Parsees, Christians, Jews, and Sikhs.

The history of the human species eloquently bears testimony to the fact that those who are especially sensitive to the sufferings of others and, being sympathetic, are impelled by an inner urge to redeem their sufferings, are peculiarly exalted not only by those who benefit from the ministry of service but also by society at large. At the age of 24, when Gandhi landed in South Africa as legal retainer for a Muslim Hindese firm, he was no better and no worse than many a contemporary barrister-at-law, Hindese or non-Hindese. But when his conscience was shocked by the injustices done to his people, when he espoused the cause of the underprivileged and the downtrodden with utter abandon, without the slightest notion of monetary reward, he began to enmesh himself in a process that was to give him inner satisfaction and raise him to the pinnacle of glory successively as "our Bhai," our Brother; as "the Mahatma," Great Soul; as "Gandhiji," revered Gandhi; as "Bapuji," Dear Father.

Here, then, are the universals in Gandhi, universals which are part of the experience of all of us—the transformation of original nature into human nature through the processes of socialization, social participation, and interaction; the development and specialization of mind, intelligence, intellect, emotion, insight, heart, soul, spirit, conscience, through participation in the cultural stream and through interaction with social forces including human beings, human interests, and human values. Giving priority to conscience, Gandhi espoused the cause of the suffering and the underprivileged with utter unselfishness and became one of the immortals of human history.

These universals, these common-human traits, take on greater meaning as we try to study and understand the specific situations that confronted Gandhi and the specific ways in which he as an individual reacted to them.

Our purpose in the present context is not to attempt a biography of Gandhi; our task will be primarily to present a psychograph as well as a sociograph of Mahatma Gandhi. By the term psychograph I mean a statement of inner processes of thinking, evaluation, and acting; while the term sociograph stands for the matrix of the social situation which defines the possibilities and limits of one's actions.

Gandhi may truly be said to be the child of One World. The title of Mr. Willkie's notable book was merely the affirmation of a situation achieved by Western civilization during the nineteenth and twentieth centuries. For a hundred years science and technology have been annihilating distances in time and space and converting the once-vast globe into a small neighborhood world. Modern methods of transportation and communication have spanned the oceans, linked countries together, and made it easy for man to travel from one part of the world to another. Gandhi's experience as a child of One World, while somewhat unique for the latter part of the nineteenth century, is the common lot of vast numbers of human beings in the twentieth century. To be born in one country (India), to study abroad (England), to labor in another country, hundreds of miles away (South Africa), to enlist the sympathetic interest of peoples yet hundreds of miles away (England, America, etc.), to undertake work in one's homeland (India) in such a way as to arouse interest and stimulate thinking among the citizens of the whole world—this indeed is a modern saga! The soldiers of all belligerent nations in World War II realized, though in a catastrophic manner, the fact of the One World in which we of the twentieth century live.

How this One World impinged upon Gandhi, how he reacted to it—this story may have some interesting object lessons for the citizens of the One World.

2. THE NON-CONFORMIST GANDHI FAMILY

Mohandas Karamchand Gandhi was born on October 2, 1869—twelve years after India's violent war of liberation whose failure earned it the title of the Sepoy Mutiny. For a generation, education had been already organized along the lines of Macaulay's note on education (1835), with an emphasis upon the English language and upon European history to the neglect of Hindese and Oriental culture. The new-fangled railroad, first introduced during the Governor-Generalship of Lord Dalhousie (1848–1856), was crisscrossing the country and making travel swifter, easier, and cheaper. The penny postcard and the reorganized postal service were making communication dependable and inexpensive. Newspapers and periodicals both in English and

in the Provincial languages had been appearing and influencing
people's thinking. English-trained lawyers in large numbers were
already beginning to "suck the blood of the poor people," [2] and
would soon be playing a prominent part in the establishment and
activities of the All-India National Congress. "Law, order, and
good government" having been securely established, the British
Raj had begun to function as the "Paramount Power" to whom
Hindese Princes, former allies of the East India Company and
of the British Crown, were called upon to pay loyalty as to a
liege-lord. Gandhi's father, uncle, and grandfather had been
associated with some of the Kathiawad states (recently integrated
into Saurashtra) as Prime Ministers.

    It certainly was not a strictly Hindu world into which Gandhi
was born; nor was it a Muslim world nor yet a European world.
Gandhi saw the light of day in a new India in the making—an
India whose past stretched back thousands of years, and yet
which stood at the threshold of a new era. With English as the
language of communication, with railroads binding the farflung
provinces of India with bands of steel, with inexpensive postal
service, with the press as the vehicle of new ideas, the stage was
set for the upsurge of political nationalism. "Law, order, and good
government" provided a fitting background for the temper of the
times in which Mohandas was born.

    For over two generations the Gandhi family had been non-
conformist professionally, though thoroughly conformist and
orthodox religiously. According to Hindu hierarchical arrangements, the Gandhis should have been plying their trade as grocers
—oil dealer, grocer, is the literal meaning of the word Gandhi.
But, as just pointed out, Gandhi's grandfather, father, and uncle
had been doing the work of administrators. Belonging as they
did to the Vaishya caste, the third order in the hierarchy, the
Gandhis were doing the work of the Kshattriya caste, the second
order in the hierarchy—a professional non-conformity which
brought prestige and wealth to the family. Religiously, however,
the Gandhi family were orthodox Hindus and devout Vaishnavas.
The Vaishnavas, who worship Vishnu as an Incarnation of God,
have many points in common with Christians in theology and in

the mode of worship. The Hindu hymn, with which Gandhi began all his major undertakings including the Salt March to Dandi, depicts the qualities of the ideal Vaishnava, the man of God; this hymn would fittingly describe the ideal Christian as well.

Rectitude, integrity, intellectual honesty—these virtues are inculcated by Hinduism most emphatically and effectively. These traits have marked those Gandhis concerning whom we have information. In addition, standing up for one's rights and for the rights of others seems to have been a special characteristic of the Gandhi family. Once, for instance, Karamchand Gandhi dared to dispute with the Assistant Political Agent, an Englishman, over the latter's reviling of the Prince; for this unheard-of defiance of British power, Prime Minister Karamchand Gandhi was arrested on the orders of the Assistant Political Agent and detained for several hours. The apology demanded by the English official was never given, and the two men later became friends.

In addition to rectitude and insistence upon rights, the Gandhi family was blessed with deep religious faith which required proper discharge of one's obligations to one's inner self, to one's fellow men, to God. His mother, in particular, appeared to Mohandas as the very embodiment of saintliness and nobility of religious living. The impression she made on him was to remain with him all through his life.

All in all Mohandas was born in favorable surroundings with one exception—he belonged to the Vaishya group, the third and lowest of the Dwija or twice-born castes. In the fluid conditions of India, this handicap would matter little.

3. THE EMERGENCE OF THE EXPERIMENTER

The evolution of Mahatma Gandhi's life points an interesting lesson. Life was conceived by Mahatma Gandhi as a field for experimentation; the purpose of the experiment on life was conceived by him to be the attainment of Truth. The methods to be used in this experiment upon life for the purpose of attaining Truth were those of the inner light, of conscience, of the still small voice within. It was Gandhi's conception that the truth or falsity in a situation had to be decided in the light of one's own conscience, not on the basis of accepted authority whether secular or sacred. Once the inner light led him to believe something to be right, Gandhi felt he was under obligation to carry out the dictates of his conscience regardless of the consequences. Throughout his life these principles have been vividly illustrated.

Let us look at two instances in his boyhood experiences. When he was a youngster attending the grade schools in the state of Kathiawad, he came in contact with boys who were of different religious persuasions. In addition to Hindus he came in contact with Muslims, Parsees, Christians, and Jews. It was common knowledge that the burly Englishman whose religion was different from that of the Hindus ate beef and all kinds of meat and did not seem to be any the worse off for it. Gandhi and his fellow students in the grade school began to think about the problem of meat-eating, even though in strict orthodox Hindu homes meat is taboo on religious grounds. Gandhi began to ask himself why the Hindus refrained from eating meat. Was it due to a special religious injunction vouchsafed to the Hindus alone and denied to the followers of other religions, or was it due to some sort of superstition? In his own immature fashion he answered these questions by saying to himself that meat-eating had nothing to do with religion, that it was perhaps an outmoded custom among the Hindus. Furthermore, it was his judgment that meat-eating gave strength to the human body. If India was going to be free, her sons and daughters ought to eat meat and then they would be a match for the beef-eating, burly Englishman. Following this train of reasoning, Gandhi was willing to try out the experiment in meat-eating. A Mohammedan fellow student would go to the meat market, buy the meat, and cook it on the banks of the river. Young Mohandas with two or three Hindu rebel boys participated, on the sly, in the experiment in meat-eating, along with the Mohammedan boy. This experiment lasted a short while and then the youngster gave it up because he thought it was unethical for him not to tell the whole truth to his mother when, after his meat supper, he was not hungry enough to do full justice to the evening meal at home. Thus the experiment in meat-eating came to an end, but it showed the mettle of the boy; he was willing to try out what his conscience told him was right and he was bold enough to discard his previous judgment if later experience proved to him that it had been wrong.

About the age of 15 to 16 young Mohandas became disturbed about religious problems. He could not find the right answers to the various questions that began to arise in his thinking and he was not quite sure that there was a God to rule over the destinies of this universe. While it is true that his father and mother were very religious, young Mahandas had no knowledge of the scriptures of his own faith or of other faiths. Thus he was thoroughly immature in matters religious and philosophical. Still groping, as he was, for an answer to the riddle of existence, he came to the conclusion that perhaps there was no guiding hand above. In desperation, Gandhi reasoned to himself: "If there be a God let him be; he does not seem to be interested in my problems. As for me, it shall be agnosticism." Later in life, especially in London while he was studying law, Gandhi became acquainted with the teachings of the Bhagavad Gita and with the teachings of the Sermon on the Mount, and he became a religious man—a man dedicated to the carrying out of the will of God. This religious agnosticism of his earlier days was a herald of the inner character of the man. Rely upon the inner light, arrive at a judgment, and abide by it regardless of the consequences—such was the emerging pattern of Gandhi's life. He was always wrestling with the problems that confronted him and finding tentative answers and acting upon them.

These two instances in Gandhi's boyhood days show the experimental attitude of the man, his reliance upon conscience, his utter disregard of conventions and customs, and his readiness to carry out the dictates of conscience, even if they went against the folkways and *mores* of society and against the scriptural injunctions of his people.

In the 1880's it was not considered right and proper for a caste Hindu to cross the "black waters." Gandhi's voyage to England in 1888 for the study of law throws further light upon the character of the youth. After graduation from high school young

Mohandas spent a year in college. In the ordinary course of events he might possibly have finished his college studies in India and served his country in his own fashion. But a novel situation intervened which was to leave an abiding impress upon the young boy and his future life. A Jain priest once talked to young Mohandas about the advisability of going to England for the study of law. He reasoned that if the youth went to England and studied law he would be able to make a name for himself and his family, amass fortune, and render service to his country. Young Mohandas was thrilled with the prospect of adventure, the prospect of going to a new land among strange people; the study of law seemed a suitable preparation if he were to offer himself for service to his people.

Two obstacles, however, stood in the way before Gandhi could go to London for the study of law. First, he had to get the consent of his mother and, second, he had to get the consent of his caste group. The elders of the caste served definite notice on the young man that if he ever went to England he would be outcasted, excommunicated. This threat did not bother Gandhi very much and it is a matter of historical interest that till his death Mohandas Karamchand Gandhi was an outcaste, so far as his particular caste community was concerned. The real problem was that of getting his mother's consent. The mother had heard all kind of wild tales concerning immorality in London, and she was afraid of letting her immature young son go to a far-off place bristling with temptations. The problem was finally solved after a great deal of persuasion and arguing on the part of Mohandas: in the presence of the Jain priest, the boy took a threefold vow to abjure the temptations of meat, wine, and sex.

Be it said to the young man's credit that he faithfully carried out this threefold vow, even though the vow concerning abstention from meat in England proved quite difficult at times. His interest in vegetarian food led Gandhi to participate in the vegetarian movement, and brought him in contact with the leaders of that movement, especially Sir Edwin Arnold, author of *The Song Celestial*, an English rendition of the Bhagavad Gita. Contrary to his mother's fears, it was in London that Gandhi had his first spiritual illumination. Let us remember that he had been an agnostic when he went to London; then in the city of London he became acquainted with the Sermon on the Mount, and with the teachings of his own sacred scripture, the Bhagavad Gita, which may be called the New Testament of Hinduism. The agnostic of yesterday now became a full believer in God, a changed man, one dedicated to the carrying out of the will of God in his own life.

Mohandas engaged in one rather humorous experiment during the early days of his sojourn in London. Under the guidance of an elderly Hindese, young Mohandas tried turning himself into an English gentleman. To that end he took lessons in dancing, in violin-playing, in French, and in elocution. He found dancing awkward. The violin lessons were meant to cultivate the ear, but cultivated only disappointment. After a few months of this experiment, the young Gandhi concluded he had been squandering money on accomplishments which were irrelevant to the study of law—or to the making of a gentleman. So he sold his violin and discontinued his lessons. Gandhi finished his law studies at the Inner Temple according to the rituals of the English law schools and was called to the bar in the year 1891. In the perspective of history Gandhi's law studies in England were less important than his contact with and participation in English culture. The English way of life made a tremendous impact upon the young, alert man from India. Consciously and unconsciously he made note of the English patterns of living, so different in so many ways from the patterns of living of his own people.

4. THE IMPACT OF WESTERN CULTURE

I have noted that in the city of London there took place what may be properly called Gandhi's first spiritual illumination. In addition, the parliamentary system of government in England and the English regard for civil liberties made a profound impression upon the youth. The intelligent and responsible participation in the making of national policies by English citizens was a novel experience to young Mohandas Gandhi. The courtesy of the London policeman was in sharp contrast to the discourtesy

of policemen in India. Even the barbers in England, he once told
a gathering of his compatriots in India, talked politics and took
part in politics. This "even" is interesting because the barbers in
India were traditionally considered not worthy to take part in
public activities! The English sense of fair play and loyalty to
freedom created in Gandhi an impression that was to abide with
him the rest of his life. But he was soon to discover in India and
later in South Africa that the English sense of fair play and devotion to freedom were not meant for export. For instance, an English official in India, whom Gandhi had known in England during his student days, was approached on the basis of personal
acquaintance by Gandhi, soon after Gandhi's return from England as a law student—with the result that he was summarily
ejected from the Englishman's house! The noble qualities of
English character, Gandhi was soon to discover, were to be practiced only in Britain and subordinated abroad to the system of
imperialism. In South Africa he discovered the insane pride of
"race" which led Englishmen and Boers alike to treat Asians and
Africans with cruelty and contempt. Exceptions to this general
practice were many and pleasant; and Gandhi was always more
than generous in acknowledging the friendship and aid of many
a noble English man and woman.

Gandhi's reaction to the growing industrialism of Britain
during his sojourn in England was negative. He came to the conclusion that the machine, instead of serving as a tool of man, was
becoming the master of man. Instead of providing promised
leisure, the machine began to exploit human beings at long and
tedious hours of work. The employment of men, women, and
children in hazardous occupations did not impress Gandhi any
more than it would anybody with the slightest sensitivity to human
values. Later, Gandhi was to conclude that industrialism must ex-
pand into imperialism, and aggression against weak nations. An
industrialized empire would exploit the vast masses of subject
territories.

Gandhi studied in England during a period of reaction
against industrialism. In the movement of protest were such
notable Englishmen as John Ruskin and William Morris. In

Russia Leo Tolstoy was preaching the simple way of life, and in America, Henry David Thoreau's influence was beginning to be felt. Those who protested against the excesses of industrialism were not obscurantists; they were moved by a profound concern for human values. The sight of ugly factories, the experience of the exploitation of human beings at starvation wages—these traits which are characteristic of infant and of growing industrialization were witnessed by Gandhi on three continents. It was his misfortune to see industrialism at its worst first in England (1888–1891), then in South Africa (1894–1914), and then in India (1915-on). These experiences set Gandhi against the cult of the machine and the worship of industrialism.

Gandhi was not opposed to the machine as machine; he was opposed to a large-scale use of machinery which tended to exploit human beings. He was quite clear in emphasizing this point in the many discussions I had with him on the subject of industrialism. He went to the length of saying to me, once, that if America or England were to solve the problem of operating large-scale machinery without entailing exploitation of human beings, he would be the first to advocate industrialism for India. The spinning wheel, the emblem of non-violent revolution in India, had both sentimental and political significance to Gandhi. He said time and again that India should win her freedom at the point of the spindle, not at the point of the bayonet.

In South Africa, too, Gandhi encountered the problems of racialism, imperialism, and nationalism. A handful of European colonists, Dutch and British, imposed their rule upon the millions of African natives. The white population, less than one-tenth of the total population, lorded it over the rest of the population. Color, assumed as the badge of inferiority, was invoked by the European colonist not only against the Africans, but also against the Asians—this, although the Hindese and the Chinese had developed arts of civilization when the Europeans were living as savages. On the foundation of gunpowder, originally invented by the Chinese for use in firecrackers, the Europeans raised a superstructure of civilization whose watchwords were violence, conquest, and exploitation.

Also, in South Africa Gandhi witnessed a clash between nationalism and imperialism, between the Boer Republic and British imperialists. He lived in South Africa long enough to see the integration of clashing nationalisms into a new nation, the Union of South Africa—a so-called democracy. It may be noted that the Union of South Africa is the first laboratory for the study of the Nazi doctrines of racialism without benefit of the Nazis themselves. The entire ideology of race superiority and of the right of might has been in operation in South Africa for over three generations.

Gandhi's stay in South Africa for two decades, in a self-imposed exile on behalf of his underprivileged countrymen, thus brought him face to face with the vital issues of the twentieth century, namely, racialism, imperialism, political or economic as well as ideological, nationalism, and exploitation. More than that, South Africa was to serve him as a laboratory for the forging of a new weapon—the weapon of non-violent resistance in the struggle of a handful of Hindese against the entrenched might of the British empire and against the government of South Africa. It was in South Africa that Gandhi read profitably the writings of Tolstoy and Thoreau. There he developed the program of non-violent resistance in accordance with the genius of his own people and the teachings of the Sermon on the Mount.

The Sermon on the Mount had made Gandhi a changed person; it had challenged him, and forced him to consider how that particular body of teachings could be made into a program of political action.

In South Africa for the first time Gandhi developed the idea of establishing a colony or Ashram as a sort of G. H. Q. for non-violent soldiers. There in South Africa, dominated by racial arrogance, Gandhi was privileged to know and have as friends many noble European men and women, as well as many politicians who were concerned primarily with power and racism. Among the notable men and women who espoused Gandhi's cause in South Africa may be mentioned Rev. and Mrs. Joseph J. Doke, Mr. and Mrs. H. S. L. Polak, Mr. and Mrs. A. H. West, and Mr. Hermann Kallenbach, a German colonist. Let me here also mention Gandhi's dealings with General Smuts, who in this episode appeared not as the wise statesman we were to see in him at the time of the Versailles Peace Conference, but as a petty politician concerned with safeguarding the privileged status of superiority for the white minority by any and every means. At that, Smuts made an abiding contribution to the literature of pacifism when he described Gandhi and his followers as "conscientious objectors."

In India proper where Gandhi labored in the full glare of publicity from January, 1915, until his martyrdom in January 1948, he met once more the problems of imperialism and nationalism. Not a small part of the resurgence of nationalism in India may be attributed to him. His people suffered from a sense of inferiority, from slave mentality. They had lost the sense of pride in the achievements of their forefathers. Under prolonged foreign rule the people had developed the habit of submitting to injustice without protest. The English-educated leadership of the national movement, Gandhi discovered, was divorced from the vast masses of people in whose behalf they claimed to labor. Gandhi's work under the circumstances was cut out for him. He had to get rid of the inferiority complex of his people. He had to infuse in them a new sense of pride for their past heritage and for the achievements they were capable of in their own day and generation. Furthermore, he had to bring the intelligentsia into direct touch with the masses. And finally, he had to emphasize to his people that resolutions as such were meaningless; resolutions, if they were to be effective, had to be backed up with sanctions. The sanctions that Gandhi would rely upon were the sanctions of non-violent resistance or of soul force.

Such in brief outline is the type of world in which Gandhi lived, labored, and died. Problems of the relations between Orient and Occident, problems of nationalism, imperialism, racialism, totalitarianism, and industrialism, all faced Gandhi; he tried to solve them in his own fashion, with India as the grand laboratory. In the process he developed the technique of non-violent resistance, the philosophy of Soul Force, or the moral equivalent of war.

CHAPTER TWO

THE MORAL EQUIVALENT OF WAR

T HE PHRASE and the concept, "the moral equivalent of war," were invented by the great American philosopher, William James. The ethical validity of moral force, in contradistinction to physical force, was preached by Leo Tolstoy. But it remained for Gandhi to work out the actual technique of the moral equivalent of war, first in South Africa on a small scale, then in India on a national scale.

Just before his death, in a prophetic letter to Gandhi (September 7, 1910) Leo Tolstoy said:

"Your activity in the Transvaal, as it seems to us at this end of the world, is the most essential work, the most important of all the work now being done in the world, wherein not only the nations of the Christian, but of all the world, will unavoidably take part."

Tolstoy's prophecy has been borne out. For the next four decades, during his lifetime, Gandhi arrested the attention of the world, and his movement came to be looked upon as a cure for a world "sick unto death of blood-spilling." [1]

1. THE GENESIS OF GANDHI'S MORAL EQUIVALENT OF WAR

Several factors account for Gandhi's development of the technique of non-violent resistance—first in South Africa and later in India. To begin with, alike in South Africa and in India, the Hindese were unarmed, incapable of offering organized violent resistance to the system of tyranny and injustice. Second, wide acquaintance with and predisposition to the practice of *dharna*, as a technique of non-violent resistance on the part of the Hindese, must be regarded as a significant factor. Third, due credit must be given to the personality of the leader himself, devoted to the Sermon on the Mount, engaged in the quest for non-violent alternatives, for the moral equivalent of war. Let us discuss these points briefly.

First: How thoroughly the Hindese people had become emasculated may be gauged from constant, plaintive reiterations by the leaders that India was too weak to offer violent resistance. Gandhi himself, who preferred non-violence to violence, never missed an opportunity to point out the degradation and unmanliness brought about by subjection to foreign rule. And in the Declaration of Independence (January 26, 1930), Gandhi, discussing "the fourfold disaster to our country," stated the fourth indictment against British rule as follows: [2]

"Spiritually, compulsory disarmament has made us unmanly, and the presence of an alien army of occupation, employed with deadly effect to crush in us the spirit of resistance, has made us think that we cannot look after ourselves or put up a defense against foreign aggression, or even defend our homes and families from the attacks of thieves, robbers and miscreants."

Pandit Jawaharlal Nehru described the Hindese of those days as "a demoralized, timid, and hopeless mass, bullied and crushed by every dominant interest, and incapable of resistance," whom Gandhi later transformed into "a people with self-respect and self-reliance, resisting tyranny, and capable of united action and sacrifice for a larger cause." [3]

Second: The doctrine of *dharna* is an integral part of Hindu philosophy and practice from ages past. *Dharna* implies the application of moral pressure to the offending party through physical austerities deliberately endured by oneself. Gandhi himself knew the stories of dharna-sitting in Porbandar, when all trade was dislocated and the physical force of the State was helpless before the irresistible power of organized non-violence.

Bishop Reginald Heber (1783–1826) in his Journal faithfully describes the practice: "To sit *dharna*, or mourning, is to remain motionless in that posture, without food, and exposed to the weather, till the person against whom it is employed consents to the request offered." [4] The present writer in his boyhood days in Palsana witnessed *dharna* successfully practised by a Muslim mendicant who, having been refused food by a Muslim merchant, stood motionless in front of the shop for over twenty-four hours.

Bishop Heber's account of one widespread *dharna* reads like a vivid account of a modern *hartal* (literally, suspension of all public activities) during Gandhi's non-violent movement for India's freedom:

"The news flew over the country like the fiery cross in *The Lady of the Lake*, and three days after it [the call for *dharna*] was issued, and before the Government were in the least apprised of the plan, above three hundred thousand persons, as it is said, deserted their houses, shut up their shops, suspended the labor of their farms, forbore to light fires, dress victuals, many of them even to eat, and sat down with folded arms and drooping heads, like so many sheep, on the plain which surrounds Benares." [5]

Third: Gandhi, the product of this cultural tradition, a daring non-conformist and a bold experimenter, put the peculiar stamp of his genius upon the theory of non-violence.

A Gujarati couplet, learned in his childhood days, profoundly influenced his conscious and subconscious thinking:

"If a man gives you a drink of water and you give him a drink in return, that is nothing;
Real beauty consists in doing good against evil."

This basic appreciation of non-violence or Soul Force was reinforced by Gandhi's acquaintance with the Sermon on the Mount. The Sermon on the Mount may well be called the technique for converting the wrongdoer—at least, so it must have appeared to the Hindu youth enraptured with his new discovery. To one studying the Sermon on the Mount, or, for that matter, the whole of the New Testament without doctrinal encrustations, the message is clear, emphatic, and practical. "Resist not evil" need not be construed to mean resigning oneself to evil with folded hands without protest; it may more appropriately be construed to mean: "Resist not evil—rather, the evildoer— violently"; Do positive things to make the evildoer question the validity of his act. In Roman times, for instance, it was customary for a Roman citizen to commandeer the services of a non-citizen. Jesus in effect said: "If he asks you to carry a load one mile, by all means carry it under duress, since that is the legal practice; but after you have carried the load one mile under compulsion, offer to carry it the second mile *of your own volition.*" This positive act is calculated to stun, to shame, and to convert the taskmaster.

The *Bhagavad Gita,* said Gandhi, "deepened the impression" made by the Sermon on the Mount, and Tolstoy's *The Kingdom of God Is Within You* "gave it permanent form." [6] It is interesting to recall that in the very first chapter of *The Kingdom of God Is Within You* Tolstoy deals with the experiences of American abolitionists, Quakers, Mennonites, and pacifists. Thus Gandhi was directly influenced by Tolstoy, but indirectly and much more definitively by the American pioneers of peace. Add to these American influences the profound impact made on Gandhi by Thoreau's *Essay on Civil Disobedience*, and we get a measure of the spiritual debt the Mahatma owed to America.

The following two passages from Thoreau's *Essay* could easily be mistaken for Gandhi's own statement:

"If a thousand men were not to pay their tax bill this year, that would not be a violent and bloody measure, as it would be to pay them and [thereby] enable the State to commit violence and shed innocent blood. This is, in fact, the definition of a peaceful revolution, if any such is possible."

"If the tax gatherer or any other public officer asks me, as one has done, 'But what shall I do?' my answer is: 'If you really wish to do anything, resign your office.' When the subject has refused allegiance and the officer has resigned his office, then the revolution is accomplished."

Among the formative influences may also be mentioned John Ruskin's *Unto This Last* and *The Crown of Wild Olive*. Ruskin's sensitivity to human suffering and his exaltation of labor made an indelible impression upon young Gandhi. From Ruskin he learned the heterodox economic doctrine that the wealth of a people consisted in its people, not in material things. "There is no wealth but life—life, including all its powers of love, of joy, and of admiration. That country is the richest which nourishes the greatest number of noble and happy human beings; that man is the richest who, having perfected the functions of his own life to the utmost, has also the widest helpful influence, both personal, and by means of his possessions, over the lives of others." [7] Nor did Ruskin's exaltation of heroism and valor fall on deaf ears: "The difference . . . existing between regiments of men associated for purposes of violence, and for purposes of manufacture . . . [is] that the former appear capable of sacrifice, the latter not; which fact is the real reason for the general lowness of estimate in which the profession of commerce is held, as compared with that of arms." [8]

Could the capacity for self-sacrifice be instilled into his people and canalized into channels other than the profession of arms? That was the challenge. Ruskin had said, "Truly, the man who does not know when to die [in defense of the sacred honor of his profession] does not know how to live." [9] Here, then, is the secret formula for the success of non-violence: If the moral equivalent of war is to be a reality, men must learn how to die heroically and non-violently in defense of their principles.

So far as is known, Gandhi was acquainted neither with William James's essay on *The Moral Equivalent of War* (1910) nor with his *Varieties of Religious Experience* (1902). He knew little of the discipline of psychology and less of sociology as taught in our colleges and universities; but, dealing as he did with human beings, striving as he did to mould heroes out of clay, Gandhi showed himself in practice a better psychologist than our professors of psychology, and superior to our professors of economics, sociology, and political science.

2. THE PSYCHOLOGY OF THE MORAL EQUIVALENT OF WAR

The psychology underlying the moral equivalent of war was pragmatically evolved by Gandhi as a result of his experiments and experiences. Man lives not by bread alone. Comfort and luxury and security cannot be the be-all and end-all of human existence. From time to time man craves the exhilaration of the heroic virtues which war brings to the fore. For the majority of mankind, the heroic virtues of disdain of personal comforts, constant alertness, readiness to lose one's life for a cause transcending one's self, are forged on the anvil of the battlefield. But the believer in non-violent resistance can forge these same heroic virtues for himself on the anvil of a moral equivalent of war, on the anvil of Satyagraha, the substitution of non-violent non-cooperation or civil disobedience for violent warfare. "The heroic virtues of disdain of personal comforts, constant alertness, readiness to lose one's life for a cause transcending one's self" are forced upon the soldier by the exigencies of battle; yet, these virtues give meaning to life, enrich life, by the compulsion of an overriding loyalty. How to develop these martial virtues in the soldier of non-violence became the crux of the problem. Gandhi's answer was simple: self-imposed poverty, voluntary renunciation of wants, self-imposed menial work, self-invited suffering. In the estimation of William James, self-imposed poverty and a voluntary renunciation of wants are conducive to heroic virtues not one whit inferior to the martial virtues.[10] Mahatma Gandhi demonstrated the validity of James's thesis.

The soldier displays his heroic martial qualities under fire. It must be pointed out, however, that the civilian who goes into the armed forces does not overnight become a heroic figure. He goes through rigid discipline. He is taught to rely more on his inward spirit and less on the trappings of civilization.

In a consecration of service to the underprivileged, to the needy, to the wronged, the civilian, too, can display the heroic virtues. The exhilaration of the heroic life, however, cannot be experienced by the civilian on a forty-hour week, on a business-as-usual basis, on hoarding, on profiteering, on racketeering, or in peaceful slumber. The civilian's experience of the heroic life depends on his ability to reorganize his mode of living, to reduce his wants, to discipline himself, to be on the alert for every opportunity for constructive work that would promote goodwill and fellowship and reconciliation, and reduce or abolish injustice, oppression, and tyranny.

Such is the psychological motivation for the moral equivalent of war. The votary of Soul Force, the soldier of non-violence, must, by will power and inner compulsion, rigidly discipline himself—his body, mind, and heart—and by constant practice learn to remain non-violent in thought, word, and deed, even under the severest provocation. He must learn to engage in right action, right as prescribed by the sense of duty, and to be detached as to the fruits of his action. By constant practice he must acquire the capacity to "reduce himself to zero," "putting himself last among his fellow-creatures." [11] He must learn to conserve, to control, anger; "as heat conserved is transmuted into energy, even so our anger controlled can be transmuted into a power which can move the world." [12] Righteous indignation against wrong, tempered by non-violence in thought, word, and deed, may generate a power mightier than the power of the sword.

Self-purification for one's own shortcomings as well as for the ills of society must be engaged in, by introspection, fasting, praying, and seeking guidance of the still small voice within. Above all, the civilian soldier of non-violence must give the utmost loyalty to Truth as he sees it. This loyalty to Truth, if it is meaningful, should lead him to revise his previous notions of right and wrong in the light of subsequent experience, if this prove necessary.

As the soldier becomes a better soldier and gains greater courage through contact and fellowship with other soldiers in the training camp or on the battlefield, so a man becomes a better soldier of non-violence if he has contact and fellowship with others of his own mode of thinking and living. Sociologists speak of the mechanisms of social interaction, social participation, and social control as conditioning human behavior. Gandhi, though innocent of a knowledge of sociology, applied its principles with intuitive skill. The Ashram, said Gandhi, shall be the non-violent soldier's training camp.

This word Ashram is one of the key words in Gandhi's life. The Ashram way of life was tried out by him in South Africa, but the word itself was first applied by him to his famous colony at Sabarmati, near Ahmedabad—*Satyagraha Ashram*. Satyagraha is made up of two words—*Satya* (Truth) and *Agraha* (Adherence). Thus *Satyagraha* means adherence to truth (and non-violence) under all circumstances. In Gandhi's thinking as in the teachings of ancient India, truth (*Satya*) and non-violence (*Ahimsa*) were inseparable, like the two sides of a coin. *Ahimsa*, which literally means non-injury, non-killing, non-violence, is always assumed to have the positive ingredient of love. The word Ashram holds a key to the understanding of ancient Hindu culture. Ashram literally means "a resting place." Historically, however, the Ashram has been a resting place, an abode, for seekers of Truth. These Ashrams were referred to as "forest hermitages" or "forest universities," because they were centers of learning and religious quest and were usually located in forests. Buddha visited several Ashrams in order to learn the Vedas, to seek the Truth, and to practise self-control. Traditionally the Ashram has stood for a peaceful abode where seekers, or disciples, live under the guidance of a *Guru* (Teacher) in order to seek and live the truth as well as to understand and practise self-control. Gandhi's Ashrams, both in South Africa and in India, emphasized seeking and living the truth (*Satya*) and inculcated self-control and self-discipline. While the ancient Ashrams aimed at individual salvation, the modern Ashrams are attuned to social service, to social salvation. Of late, several Christian leaders in India and America have been adopting the Ashram pattern of living in their religious quest. I can best describe Gandhi's Ashram as a sort of permanent religious retreat with an emphasis on the social gospel. The mass movements of protest under Gandhi's leadership, alike in South Africa and in India, may be appropriately referred to either as *Satyagraha* or as *Ahimsa*.

3. The Ashram as the G. H. Q. of Non-Violence

In 1904 Gandhi established his first Ashram at Phoenix, near Durban, in the Province of Natal, South Africa. This Phoenix Ashram was a direct result of his reading of *Unto This Last*, which drove home to Gandhi the following three lessons:

1. That the good of the individual is contained in the good of all.

2. That a lawyer's work has the same value as the barber's, inasmuch as all have an equal right to earn a livelihood from their work.

3. That the life of labor, i.e., the life of the tiller of the soil and of the handicraftsman, is the life worth living.

"The first of these," says Gandhi, "I knew. The second I had dimly realized. The third had never occurred to me. *Unto This Last* made it as clear as daylight for me that the second and the third were contained in the first. I arose with the dawn, ready to reduce these principles to practice." [13]

Indian Opinion, a weekly magazine, published in English, Tamil, Gujarati, and Hindese, which Gandhi had been editing and subsidizing, was losing money. In a twelvemonth period it had cost him £2,000, and he now decided to establish his Phoenix Ashram as much to cultivate the simple life for himself and his associates as to cut down the expenses of the weekly paper. A hundred acres of agricultural land were purchased at Phoenix, near Durban. The printing press and *Indian Opinion* were transferred to "an iron building" erected on the grounds within a month. With the workers associated with *Indian Opinion* as a nucleus, a colony grew up at Phoenix devoted to simple living. Houses were built, mostly by their own labor; land began to be cultivated; gardens made their appearance, and a school was started. Gandhi's official residence was at Phoenix, whither he would retire for brief intervals after his harassing toil in Johannesburg. His second son, Manilal Gandhi, has remained at Phoenix, editing *Indian Opinion* and carrying on the work of the non-violent warrior practically since the father's departure from South Africa.

The settlers at Phoenix were divided into two classes—share-holders who had an interest in the scheme, and paid workers. Each member received a monthly allowance of £3. The share-holders were granted in addition an acre of land with a building, which they would pay for in due course of time. Everybody contributed his labor to the soil and to as many crafts as possible; in spare time they worked on *Indian Opinion.*

These dreams—*Indian Opinion* and the Phoenix Settlement —in the words of Gandhi's first biographer, "absolutely impoverished the dreamer. What *Indian Opinion* has not required, Phoenix has. To meet these demands, however, is part of his conception of duty, and in such self-sacrifice, bringing poverty with it, he is true to his ideal." [14] At the height of his career as a barrister, Gandhi used to earn five to six thousand pounds a year; yet when he returned to India in 1915, he was practically penniless.

In conformity with the tenets of the simple life, Gandhi at first thought of running the printing press entirely with manual labor. It soon became evident that at least an "oil-engine" was necessary. When the engine would fail, the men would literally put their shoulders to the wheel, and turn out *Indian Opinion* on time. For his part, Gandhi thought hand-power "more in keeping with the atmosphere where agricultural work too was to be done by hand."

Such was the first training camp for soldiers of non-violence, the spiritual G.H.Q. It was to play a leading part in the non-violent struggle for justice by the Hindese in South Africa.

The second Ashram, called Tolstoy Farm, was established in 1910 on eleven hundred acres of land belonging to Gandhi's friend and coworker, Hermann Kallenbach. Tolstoy Farm was at Lawley, twenty-one miles from Johannesburg. All Satyagrahists (devotees of non-violence) who had taken part in the movement, and their families, made up the Ashram. Men and women lived in different blocks in dormitory-like houses. Every type of work from cooking to scavenging was done by the members themselves; there were no paid servants. The diet was vegetarian by common agreement. Alcohol and smoking were forbidden. Farming and handicrafts were the main industries. Gandhi learned how to make sandals—this was in addition to his other accomplishments as a farmer, gardener, barber, launderer, cleaner and presser, sweeper and scavenger, and as a teacher. As a teacher Gandhi had to deal with students who differed widely in age and in religious background. To discharge his duties properly, he tried to acquaint himself with the main tenets and history of the different religions observed in India.

Farm members cut each other's hair. Women were in charge of cooking and tailoring. All wore men's trousers and shirts of coarse blue cloth, as a reminder of prison uniform. Three meals were served daily, and after the evening meal, congregational worship was held at seven. They sang *bhajans* (Hindu hymns) and read from the Ramayana or from books on Islam. Everyone retired at 9:00 P.M. Most members fasted on their respective religious days.

The colony had not even the commonest medical remedies because of Gandhi's belief in nature cure. Results of experiments in diet, healing, and nature cure were set forth by Gandhi in a small book: *Guide to Health*. Writing about these experiments in nature cure, fifteen years later, Gandhi said he would "shudder" and "not venture to employ the same treatment."

Rules for simple living at Tolstoy Farm were meticulously laid down and strictly observed. Life was ordered so as to instill hardihood and breed the heroic virtues of disdain for personal comforts. It was an ideal flight from the temptations of city life. But the lure of the city could not be completely curbed. Business reasons might require a visit to nearby Johannesburg, or a trip might be taken merely for relaxation and pleasure. Hence it was agreed that "no one could travel by rail except on direct public business connected with our little commonwealth. Then, too, if we went on public business we had to travel third class. Anyone who wanted to go on a pleasure trip must go on foot, and carry homemade provisions with him. None must spend anything on his food in the city. . . . By this discipline we were able to avoid all waste of public funds." [15] Gandhi himself acquired great capacity for physical labor, and he could walk as much as 55 miles a day.

4. THE GREAT MARCH: NON-VIOLENCE IN ACTION

In the final phases of the struggle against the Government of the Union of South Africa, Gandhi transferred all the Satyagrahists from Tolstoy Farm to Phoenix, to be ready to offer non-violent resistance at the appropriate moment. The outstanding issues were five:

1. The validity of Hindu, Muslim, and Parsee marriages.

2. Abolition of the three-pound annual tax on indentured Hindese laborers who wished to remain in Natal at the end of their indenture.

3. Cessation of indentured labor from India to South Africa.

4. Free movement of Hindese from one Province of the Union to another.

5. Removal of the anti-Asiatic bias from the immigration law.

Hindese women in the Transvaal took the lead. They courted imprisonment by token violations of certain minor laws. Then they crossed the border into Natal and issued a call to the Hindese miners of Newcastle to strike. The strike spread, and three to four thousand Hindese miners, indentured laborers all, converged on the prearranged camp at Newcastle. Gandhi rushed to Newcastle from Phoenix.

On October 30, 1913, "at the head of his tattered army" of 2,037 men, 127 women, and 57 children, to quote C. F. Andrews, "he [Gandhi] began his famous march." The immediate objective was Charlestown, near the Transvaal border, where a vast camp had been organized. Gandhi telegraphed to the Government his intention to cross the border of the Transvaal with his "army," thus openly violating the law against free movement of indentured laborers. In the meantime, some agents of the Government and of the employers began to coerce and injure the indentured laborers; but these unlettered followers of Gandhi stood their ground.

At the Transvaal border Gandhi stepped forward to interview the sentry on duty. An eyewitness described the scene thus: [16] "Whilst these official preliminaries were in train, the main body became impatient, and a mass of cheering, shouting Indians, clad in ragged clothes, and bearing their pitifully small belongings upon their heads, swarmed through the streets of Volksrust, determined to do or die, brushing the handful of police aside like so many helpless and insignificant atoms. They encamped on the farther side of the town, and the great march had commenced. The program was to march at the rate of some twenty-five miles a day, until either the men were arrested or Tolstoy Farm, at Lawley, near Johannesburg, was reached. The Government were informed of each stopping-place. Eight days were set aside to reach their destination, unless they were earlier arrested, and from the swing and energy of their marching it was plain that a phenomenal feat was being performed by men, many of them heavily burdened, unused to conditions of 'war,' but accustomed to a hard and simple life, and on a meagre and unusual diet. That night they reached Palmford, where special accommodation was offered to Mr. Gandhi, who, however, refused to accept hospitality which his humbler countrymen could not share."

Gandhi's own description of the Great March is interesting: [17] "During the last stages, it [the Satyagraha movement] took a most unexpected and brilliant turn. . . . At one time nearly 30,000 men were on strike. . . . They wanted to fill the prisons. After due notice to the Government, nearly two thousand of them, men, women and children, marched into the Transvaal. They had no legal right to cross the border. Their destination was Tolstoy Farm . . .; the distance to be covered was 150 miles. No army ever marched with so little burden. No wagons or mules accompanied the party. Each one carried his own blankets and daily rations, consisting of one pound of bread and one ounce of sugar. This meagre ration was supplemented by what Indian [i.e., Hindese] merchants gave them on their way. The Government imprisoned the leaders, i.e., those they thought to be leaders. But they soon discovered that all were leaders. So when they were nearly within reach of their destination, the whole party was arrested. Thus their object [to get arrested] was accomplished."

Twice Gandhi was arrested and each time he was released on bail. Gandhi was arrested a third time, however, on November 9, 1913, near Balfour when three long trains drew up at a siding and the whole "army" was taken back to Natal and imprisoned. The prisons of Natal became overcrowded, and other forms of imprisonment—concentration camps—had to be devised. Physical coercion failed to overpower Hindese non-violence and determination. Gandhi, who had been sentenced to nine months' rigorous imprisonment at Dundee (November 11, 1913) and to three months' rigorous imprisonment on a second count at Volks-rust (November 17, 1913), was detained in Bloemfontein, capital of Orange Free State, in order to isolate him from his followers.

Force unavailing, Gandhi was released on December 18, 1913, to carry on negotiations with General Smuts for a final settlement.

"Let us put all our cards on the table so that *this time* there may be no misunderstanding in the future," said General Smuts. "My cards are always on the table," Gandhi replied. The major injustices from which the Hindese suffered were rectified, first by negotiation and later by legislation. So ended the heroic saga of the Great March, a triumph of non-violence over violence, of spirit over matter, and a demonstration of the validity of the moral equivalent of war.

CHAPTER THREE

SOUL FORCE—DESIGN FOR LIVING

1. Principles of Great Leadership

GANDHI, the great experimenter, having evolved the technique of non-violent resistance and the philosophy of Soul Force in South Africa, was nostalgic for his Motherland, the land of his ideals. There he would strive for the nearest approach to perfection. By 1909, in his *Hind Swaraj* he had outlined his conception of *Swaraj*—civilization, education, Soul Force versus brute force—and promulgated a program of action. The Non-Violent Non-Cooperation movement of the twenties was but a materialization of the ideas expressed in the book.[1]

This man who specialized in fasting and made a fetish of simple living is responsible for the modernization of India, for the healthy growth of its nationalism. When he returned to India in 1915, after a self-imposed exile of two decades, Gandhi discovered that his people had been "victimized" by English education. They had developed a slave mentality; they were overburdened with fear; they had lost the capacity to say "No" and had, therefore, become hypocritical. To redeem a whole people from such degradation is no mean accomplishment.

At heart a religious man, Gandhi was inevitably drawn into politics. In South Africa he once said to his friend Mr. Doke: "Most religious men I have met are politicians in disguise; I, however, who wear the guise of a politician, am at heart a religious man." In his quest for the Supreme Soul, Gandhi could not overlook the affairs of humanity. In his own words: "I am part

30

and parcel of the whole, and I cannot find Him apart from the rest of humanity. My countrymen are my nearest neighbors. They have become so helpless, so resourceless, so inert that I must concentrate on serving them. If I could persuade myself that I should find Him in a Himalayan cave, I would proceed there immediately. But I know that I cannot find Him apart from Humanity." [2]

Thus Gandhi was foreordained to take part in politics, to serve his fellow men. But desire to serve, even when fortified by a philosophic belief, avails nothing if the fitness to serve be missing or inadequate. The *Bhagavad Gita* had taught him the doctrine of *adhikara* or fitness. Gandhi's immediate task was, therefore, to make himself fit to serve others. The only way he knew he could make himself fit for such service was by regulating his life according to the ancient Ashram pattern, which he had so effectively experimented with in South Africa. The *Satyagraha* Ashram at Sabarmati, near Ahmedabad, founded in 1916, was to serve as a training camp for himself and his associates and as headquarters for India's non-violent revolution. The members of the Ashram took eight vows: (1) truthfulness, (2) *Ahimsa* (non-violence: love), (3) celibacy, (4) control of the palate, (5) non-thieving, (6) non-possession, (7) *Swadeshi* (encouragement of home industries), and (8) fearlessness. Education was imparted through the medium of the languages of India, English being taught as a secondary language. The dignity of manual labor was stressed, and students were taught handicrafts, especially spinning and weaving. Distinctions of caste and creed were brushed aside. Politics, economics, and sociology were taught "in a religious spirit."

India's non-violent revolution was inspired from this Ashram when on March 12, 1930, accompanied by seventy-eight Ashramites including the present writer, Mahatma Gandhi set forth on his famous March to the Sea. Gandhi told me that he undertook this March to the Sea, first, as a pilgrimage; second, to get the people's blessing; third, to initiate the non-violent revolution against the British Raj by violating the Salt Law after arrival at Dandi Beach. It was a pathetic company, these Gandhi

volunteers who did not even walk properly—either single-file or
in two's or three's. A bit of army discipline might have helped us.
As it was, what we lacked in color and finesse was more than
made up for by the presence of the man in the loin-cloth. In his
dramatization of non-violent war, Gandhi appreciated the utility
of spectacle, parade, mass attraction. Tens of thousands came to
see this March and to hear the Mahatma's speeches at various
stops.

There is something impressive and dynamic about large
groups doing the same thing in unison. Gandhi's Great March in
South Africa and his March to the Sea in India roused an exhilaration, albeit non-violent, such as would be felt by an army
marching off to war. These marches generated power—power in
Gandhi's volunteers, power in the Hindese bystanders and neu-
trals, power in the masses.

This technique of generating power may be used legitimately
and successfully by anybody, regardless of race and clime, provided the cause be just. For instance, the threat of a "March on
Washington," issued by A. Philip Randolph, President of the
Pullman Porters Union, was sufficient to induce President Roose-
velt to enforce the policy of employment of workers in war industries without discrimination against minorities in our population.
The F. E. P. C. (Fair Employment Practices Commission) was a
direct result of the new policy. Likewise did the Germans in the
Ruhr successfully practise non-violent resistance against the
French occupation authorities at the end of World War I. Our
sit-down strikes, in the late thirties, by the C. I. O. may also be
traced to Gandhi's movement—with this difference, that the
Gandhi philosophy would have had no truck with violence either
to non-striking workers or to machinery. Our C. I. O. unionists did
and do unfortunately to this day indulge in violence, though I
understand non-communist union leaders are opposed to violence
in any form.

How did Gandhi generate power for himself, to make himself fit for the leadership of his people? With becoming modesty
he answered: "Fates decide my undertakings for me. I never go
to seek them. They come to me almost in spite of me. That has

been my lot all my life long." [3] That is not quite an accurate analysis, even though it correctly points out the sociological truth that the leader is the product of his times and of circumstances surrounding him. I shall attempt my own analysis of how and why Gandhi succeeded in generating powers of leadership unmatched in human history.

As an experimenter with life, he had early concluded that true life must be lived within the framework of the twin principles, *Satya* (Truth) and *Ahimsa* (Non-Violence: Love). All else followed from this. Add a third principle—concern for the well-being of others, especially of the underprivileged, the wronged, and the oppressed—and we have the basic requirements for great leadership. The eightfold vow at the Satyagraha Ashram can be traced to one or other of these principles.

Concern for the well-being of others is, for instance, translated into the vow of non-thieving: [4] "I suggest that we are thieves in a way. If I take anything that I do not need for my immediate use, and keep it, I thieve it from somebody else . . . If somebody else possesses more than I do, let him. But so far as my own life has to be regulated, I do say that I dare not possess anything which I do not want. In India we have three millions of people * having to be satisfied with one meal a day, and that meal consisting of a chapatti containing no fat in it, and a pinch of salt. You and I have no right to anything that we really have until these three millions are clothed and fed better. You and I, who ought to know better, must adjust our wants, and even undergo voluntary starvation, in order that they may be nursed, fed and clothed." *Swadeshi, i.e.,* encouragement and use of home industries, likewise springs from a concern for the well-being of millions of Hindese who are idle for want of work.

Living as he did, devoted to truth, non-violence, and concern for others, it was inevitable that Gandhi should find plenty of evil situations at hand. Operating as he did within his chosen framework, it was inevitable that Gandhi should do something to redeem the wrongs. He had no need to seek undertakings; the invitation to undertakings was implicit in his philosophy of life.

* Thirty millions, some authorities used to say.—H.T.M.

Thus, in addition to the cause of India's freedom, either successively or simultaneously, Gandhi espoused the following causes: justice for his disfranchised compatriots in South Africa; "communal" unity among different religious groups; the Ashram way of life; the plight of third class passengers in India; impediments against free trade in certain sections of Kathiawad; the sad condition of the plantation workers in Bihar, of the famine-stricken farmers of Bardoli, of the textile workers of Ahmedabad. Also the encouragement of spinning-wheel and cottage industries; a crusade against untouchability; the emancipation of women; the promotion of the languages of India and of a national Hindese language; basic education for India's poverty-stricken millions. Some of these reforms were of a minor and passing nature, others would amount to social revolution.

The true leader discovers a challenge in existing conditions crying for change; the mediocre man—which means the majority of mankind—fails to discover any such challenge. The leader rises above the circumstances of his day; the average person submits to them. The leader strives to bring the situations into conformity with his ideals; the average person conforms to the situations.

Religious leadership is characterized by all three attributes we witness in Gandhi: *Satya, Ahimsa,* and concern for others. Buddha and Jesus aptly illustrate these three principles, *leading to action.* Philosophic leadership also illustrates these three principles, but without relation to action. William James's philosophy of pragmatism seems to be the sole exception. Secular leadership —whether political, social, economic, or intellectual—is apt to be characterized by the third principle, concern for the well-being of others. No general would be considered a hero if he recklessly sacrificed his men. Which figures in politics are venerated as great by their contemporaries and remembered as leaders by posterity? Only those who showed concern for the well-being of others.

Having discussed Gandhi's mode of operation, we must now look into his way of life. Gandhi's way of life is not meant only for heroes; it can be practised by the humblest human being; indeed, its adoption transforms the average person into a hero. What is the framework of Gandhi's way of life, his philosophy of Soul Force? Unfortunately, Gandhi was so deeply engrossed in living the life that he had no time—or inclination—to describe the motivation behind that life. We cannot understand Gandhi's philosophy of Soul Force without reference to his Hindu background and to the influence of Christ's teachings.

2. THE PHILOSOPHY OF SOUL FORCE

Soul Force may be viewed from four different angles; or, better yet, it may be viewed at four different levels. First and foremost, Soul Force is the primeval element pervading the universe. Here there is no possibility of conflict because of man's communion with Soul Force at the highest level. Second, Soul Force is a way of life in harmony with the cosmic process. There is no possibility of conflict at this second level, either, because of harmony with the cosmic process. Third, Soul Force is a tool of spiritual insight into the workings of the universe of which we are all integral parts. Here there is the possibility of conflict because of man's freedom to choose the tools of insight. Fourth and least important, if the conflict is not resolved at the third level by the right choice, Soul Force manifests itself as a technique for resolving crises and conflict situations. In this context, the term conflict is used to signify tension. At the first level, tension would imply estrangement of the human soul from the Supreme Soul. At the second level, it would mean disharmony with the cosmic process; at the third level, ideological differences; and, at the fourth level, violent hostilities.

1. *Soul Force as the Cosmic Principle.* Soul Force as the cosmic principle has been known to mankind, East and West, from times immemorial. Soul Force is the primeval energy, the creative spirit, the self-existent Being without beginning and without end. Prophets have exalted it and poets have sung of its glory. Some refer to Soul Force as a He, some as a She, some as an It: they all mean the same thing. In the Infinitude of the Supreme Being, sex, gender, and age become meaningless. Call it the primeval substance or the form of the formless; call it the Ding-an-sich or the

Thing-in-itself (of Kant) if you will; call it the interplay of matter and spirit; call it the Brahma; call it the Oversoul as Emerson did—call it by what name you will, Soul Force is the beginningless, the endless, the only *Satt* (Sanskrit: Being or Truth) that is infallible in the universe. And to the extent that the elements of the universe—galaxies and planets, atoms and electrons, birds, beasts, and men—are a part of the *Satt,* do they partake of the nature of the divine. Under this condition alone do the sentient creatures realize their identity, their at-one-ness, with the Supreme *Satt* (Supreme Being: Supreme Truth). *Satt* manifests itself in terms of *Chitt* (Sanskrit: Mind or Intelligence) and culminates in *Ananda* (Sanskrit: Joy or Bliss).

Defying the compulsions of matter, rising above the prison-walls of institutions, holding fast to his inner being in the midst of the *Maya* (illusion) of processes, man can truly affirm and realize with Jesus, "I and My Father are one"; or, with Buddha, "I have become the Awakened, the Enlightened, one."

Experiencing Soul Force at the highest level, as mystics have done, man can obliterate differences and conflicts from his behavior as well as from his consciousness.

2. *Soul Force in Tune with the Cosmic Process.* Soul Force is a way of life in tune with the cosmic process. The fundamental oneness of life is the essential aspect of this universe of ours. The stars and the planets move in their appointed orbits; the trees blossom forth into magnificent foliage and flowers; the birds chirp and teeter on the boughs, bedecked in pleasing plumage; the rivers flow majestically, unconcerned with the passing show; the oceans retain their gravity and serenity the while receiving untold amounts of water from rivers; nature evolves from the simple to the complex, favoring one form and discarding another—all these events in the universe are but manifestations of Soul Force, of God if you prefer the term. Man's supreme happiness consists in the realization of his oneness with the rest of creation.

Aham Brahma-Asmi, I AM BRAHMA, is but a variant of the other saying: *Tat-Twam-Asi,* i.e., THAT THOU ART. I am Brahma. You are Brahma. I am That. You are That. Your highest bliss and mine, then, consists in our being in communion with That. Hence the injunction: "Thou shalt love the Lord thy God with all thy heart, with all thy soul, and with all thy mind."

Again, if you are That and if I too am That, then you and I have a fundamental affinity, one with another. Indeed, you, my neighbor, are myself in another form; and I am yourself in another form. Hence the injunction: "Thou shalt love thy neighbor as thyself."

Ecstatic devotion to the Most High or supreme adoration of the Ultimate Reality, and realization of the identity of oneself with one's neighbors—these two requirements of the inner life of the spirit flow naturally from Soul Force.

The corollary is obvious: "The virtue of that life and power" (Soul Force) must "take away the occasion of all wars." The indwelling Light of Soul Force not only "leads out of wars, leads out of strife, leads out of the occasion of wars, and leads out of the earth up to God, and out of earthly mindedness into heavenly mindedness"; it also puts upon us the obligation of *Ahimsa* (non-violence: love).

Here Hindu metaphysic and Christian teaching, as expounded by George Fox, meet in majestic confluence like the Jumna and the Ganges.

There is no possibility of conflict at this second level of Soul Force because of harmony with Soul Force at the first level.

3. *Soul Force as a Tool of Spiritual Insight.* Soul Force embraces the totality of being. Hence it serves the purpose of what the scientists call "a frame of reference." No event occurring in the universe is outside the purview of this frame of reference. Indeed, Soul Force serves admirably as a criterion for judging events and actions, or as an integrating principle. To Mahatma Gandhi it is "an angle of vision." In the language of empiricism it is a hypothesis. The hypothesis of Soul Force postulates that the universe is hospitable, friendly, loving. In Plato's terminology, the universe may be conceived as the quintessence of the good, the true, the beautiful.

Opposed to the theory of Soul Force, there is the postulate of Brute Force being at the core of the universe. This latter theory holds that the universe is inhospitable, unfriendly, unloving, at best amoral if indeed not immoral. This view is well expressed in the Hindu dialectician's phrase *Matsya-Nyaya*, "the logic of the fish" —"the larger fish devouring the smaller fish."

In Occidental thought this point of view was best set forth by Hobbes, Malthus, and Darwin. Hobbes defined the state of nature as "a struggle of each against all." Malthus premised that population tended to outstrip the food supply; thus there ensued the struggle for existence. Darwin studied nature and arrived at the conclusion that there was universal "struggle for existence"; that only "the fittest" survived, giving rise to new species.

Interestingly enough, another student of nature, Prince Peter Kropotkin of Russia, arrived at the conclusion that in nature there was "mutual aid."

Darwin and Kropotkin are both partly right and partly wrong. In nature we have both phenomena: the struggle for existence, and mutual aid. To read in nature exclusively a struggle for existence, or exclusively mutual aid, would be wrong. We must balance the two in terms of the fundamental frame of reference. The experience of nature as well as of man, an integral part of nature, points to an interesting lesson. In the struggle for existence, that species which learned cooperation and mutual aid among its members has succeeded, survived, and prospered. Benjamin Kidd is quite right when he suggests that social progress consists in the capacity for teamwork, in the capacity of the individual member to subordinate himself to the group. Self-preservation, accordingly, becomes group preservation. One finds one's true self when one is willing to lose it for others. How perfectly is the teaching of religion in harmony with the findings of science! But we can arrive at this conclusion because we are operating within the frame of reference of Soul Force.

Contrariwise, the frame of reference of Brute Force compels different conclusions. Man must be eternally at war with nature and with his fellows. To survive, he must be aggressive and brutal. The more brutal he is, the more likely is he to survive —and to dominate. He must therefore glorify war and create occasions for war. In the war of each against all, there can be no mutual trust, no confidence, no tenderness, in human relations. Man must not only build engines of human destruction; he must himself be an engine of Brute Force.

Hobbes, Malthus, and Darwin, honored social philosophers and scientists as they were, have been responsible to no small extent for the cult of brute force in Western civilization, for "the white man's burden" upon "the lesser breed," for racialism, and for imperialism. In our day, Marxism reinforces the philosophy of violence and brute force.

Granted these two possible approaches to an understanding of nature, which one shall we choose as a guide to our behavior— Soul Force or Brute Force?

The Hindus speak of *Rajju-Sarpa-Nyaya*, "the logic of the rope-snake." If in the dim twilight of an evening you should chance upon a rope lying on the road and think it is a serpent, your reaction to the object would be conditioned by your *belief* that it is a snake. That, objectively, it is a mere piece of rope is immaterial; to you at the moment *it is a snake*. And your response is watchfulness, and either a fight or a flight.

The German philosopher Vaihinger developed the same notion in his concept of *Als ob*, "As if." Man's response to the environment is not in terms of the objective reality but in terms of his subjective conception of the situation.

Granted the universe were unfriendly—an untenable assumption—how about man responding to it *as if* it were hospitable? Could not man by his very response transform the nature of the cosmic process? But we are not compelled to battle against the universe. The universe *is* friendly and hospitable. It is our view of the universe that needs to be harmonized with the ultimate nature of Soul Force.

Because man is free to choose as a guide to his conduct either of the two frames of reference, Brute Force or Soul Force, at this level of Soul Force there is the possibility of conflict.

4. *Soul Force a Technique for Resolving Conflicts*. If in spite of man's best attempt to live at the first three levels of Soul Force conflict does arise, then he must translate Soul Force into a technique for resolving crises and conflict-situations.

To Mahatma Gandhi, in our age, belongs the credit for having worked out Soul Force as a technique for resolving crises and conflict-situations. The technique of Soul Force or *Satyagraha* (i.e., insistence upon Truth under all circumstances) can be effectively used by a single individual as well as by a group of people large or small.

The theory is so simple that even a child can understand it. Fellowship among human beings is possible on two planes—the plane of joy and the plane of suffering. On either plane man becomes oblivious of his petty self and realizes his kinship with the Supreme Self, with Soul Force.

A simple illustration of kinship on the plane of joy is afforded by recreation. Abiding by the rules of the game, the players enjoy a fellowship which is no part of the routine activities of this humdrum life. Group recreation, either indoors or outdoors, is a tonic to the spirit, precisely because participants in recreation experience joy and fellowship on the common-human level.

The inner man is touched by suffering as well as by joy. The occurrence of an accident does not call forth the response: What is his nationality? Does he go to church regularly? How shabbily dressed is he? No, none of these accidental trappings of man's self engages our attention. The prompt response is always: Is he badly hurt? What can we do for him?

There is then this basic law of human behavior: The inner self in each man is touched by joy as well as by suffering and is transported into common fellowship with the object of joy or of suffering. Gandhi understood intuitively this basic law of human behavior.

Suffering calls forth a realization of common-human kinship. Why not then, in effect argued the Mahatma, utilize the technique of "self-invited suffering" to call forth the response of common-human kinship from those that persecute and exploit us and deny us justice and freedom?

Soul Force posits a divine potential in the wrongdoer, be he British, or German, or whatever he may be. And it is this divine potential, the inner man, within the wrongdoer that must be touched and "coerced" to respond to "self-invited suffering." The wrongdoing itself is the logical end-product of an encrusted system or institution—the Empire System, for example—which enslaves the wrongdoer as well as the wronged. Hence the wrongdoer must be made to see the injustice of the system, to question the validity of the system he operates, by the victim inviting suffering upon himself in the spirit of *Ahimsa* (non-violence: love). The concrete technique of Soul Force has been named *Satyagraha* (holding fast to Truth) by Gandhi.

That the political movement of non-violent non-cooperation, or of civil disobedience, was motivated by some such philosophy of Soul Force needs to be emphasized: "I have no God to serve but Truth." [5] Again, "I can easily put up with the denial of the world, but any denial by me of my God is unthinkable." [6]

The relation between God and Truth fascinated Mahatma Gandhi ever since maturity. In Geneva, the birthplace of Calvinism, the Mahatma discussed Truth and God in refreshing terms. "Until now," said Gandhi, "I used to say 'God is Truth.' Now I believe Truth is God." The statement "God is Truth" is partial, contends Gandhi; the statement "Truth is God" is all-inclusive.

Truth is unrealizable except in terms of *Ahimsa,* that is to say, except in terms of non-violence and love. *Ahimsa* is to be viewed not merely as a grand principle, but *as the way of life.* To complete Gandhi's chain of reasoning we must recall the ancient Sanskrit saying: *Satyaméva Jayaté,* i.e., TRUTH ALONE CONQUERS!

3. SOUL FORCE INVOLVES BOTH COOPERATION AND NON-COOPERATION

In spite of its revolutionary character, *Satyagraha* has a great affinity with democracy; I suppose, because democracy, too, was born of revolution and has dynamic capacity for effecting change of the most revolutionary type in a peaceful manner.

It is unbecoming to the dignity of man supinely to submit to injustice and wrong. In order to abolish existing injustice and wrong the Satyagrahist studies the system or systems and patterns that make for wrong and injustice. He would try to mend or to end, "to alter or to abolish," the system that is responsible for wrongdoing. In his zest to eliminate the wrong, the Satyagrahist is ever careful not to eliminate the wrongdoer. *Satyagraha* does not aim to cure the rash without cleansing the whole system. If a purge be necessary, let there be a purge—a non-violent purge, to be sure. The Satyagrahist looks behind the flutter of phenomena.

The Satyagrahist gives the benefit of the doubt to his antagonist; he strives generously to understand the other's point of view. He cooperates whenever cooperation involves no compromise with principle, with Truth. He works for conciliation and arbitration. His concern is not only to minimize conflict but also to minimize the occasions for conflict.

Democracy is based upon Soul Force; indeed, the democratic process is *par excellence* the manifestation of Soul Force in action; because democracy, too, strives to minimize conflict and occasions for conflict.

The role of self-invited suffering is most important in the technique of *Satyagraha*. Non-cooperation with the agency of wrongdoing in turn depends upon cooperation among the "revolutionaries." Only self-purification and prosecution of the constructive program make the people fit to offer non-cooperation.

When goodwill and conciliation are unavailing, the Satyagrahist who foreswore violence and warfare has open to him only one course of action, namely, to invite upon his devoted head all the sufferings he can without malice, without ill-will. Sensitivity to suffering is the hallmark of humanity. Hence by inviting suffering upon ourselves we may light up the spark of the divine potential in the wrongdoer.

The process of inviting suffering upon one's self takes two forms: (1) self-purification, internally; and (2) non-cooperation with the agency of wrongdoing, externally.

Self-purification is meant both for the individual and for society. The Satyagrahist must not hesitate to take upon himself and upon his society, upon his nation, part of the responsibility for existing wrongs. Acts of self-purification call for a reconditioning of the individual and a mending or an ending of internal patterns and systems and institutions that inflict injustice and wrong upon society as a whole or upon certain sections of society. To that end soldiers of non-violence *cooperate* one with another and with other members of society to rid themselves of internal social wrongs.

This is one part of *Satyagraha—the constructive program* based upon self-purification and internal cooperation.

The other part of *Satyagraha* is non-cooperation with the agency or system that is responsible for the major wrong or injustice in society.

Concretely speaking, in India *Satyagraha* involved, on the one hand, the fivefold constructive program:

(1) Hindu-Muslim unity,
(2) Abolition of untouchability,
(3) Prohibition of narcotics and liquor,
(4) The greater participation of women in the nation's fight for freedom,
(5) The encouragement of home industries, such as spinning, weaving, and handicrafts of all sorts.

On the other hand, it involved non-cooperation with the British Government and its institutions:

(1) Renunciation of titles,
(2) Non-participation in official functions,
(3) Non-cooperation with government courts and schools, and the setting up of people's courts and national schools,
(4) Non-violent violation of predetermined laws of the government and seeking arrest and imprisonment,
(5) Peaceful picketing of government-licensed opium and liquor shops,
(6) Non-cooperation with the civil and military administration of the country,
(7) Non-payment of taxes.

Gandhi devised the program of non-cooperation not as a substitute for cooperation with the British Raj; he devised it as a substitute for irresponsible, sporadic violence which would have engulfed India as part of the natural cycle of nationalist upsurge. Thus, within the framework of his philosophy of Soul Force, Mahatma Gandhi proved the efficacy of the moral equivalent of war.

CHAPTER FOUR

THE MAHATMA AND THE POET

IN THE first half of the twentieth century the Hindese scene was dominated by two outstanding figures, strikingly similar in their love of Mother India but diametrically opposed to each other in their behavior patterns. Rabindranath Tagore, scion of an aristocratic Brahmin family, the poet laureate of India, expressed his love of India in terms of cooperation with the Western world. Mahatma Gandhi, the man of simple prose and energetic action, born of a Vaishya family, lover of unadorned truth, expressed his love of India in terms of non-cooperation with the Western world, especially with the British Raj. Tagore was born in Bengal, long the intellectual center of India, famous for a galaxy of towering personalities in religion, art, literature, politics, and revolutionary activities. Gandhi was born in Gujarat, an unspectacular province of hard-working farmers and keen businessmen, unconcerned with politics, and having no truck with violence or revolutionary activity of any kind.

Tagore's intellectual lineage included such stalwarts in the life of the spirit as Ram Mohan Roy (1772–1833), the Maker of Modern India and founder of the Brahmo Samaj; Ramakrishna Paramahamsa (1836–1886), Keshab Chandra Sen (1838–1884), Swami Vivekananda (1862–1902); his own grandfather, Dwarkanath Tagore (died 1846) and his father, Devendranath (1817–1905), known as the Maharshi, the Great Rishi. Tutored at home, as befitted the scion of an aristocratic family, Tagore escaped the hybrid system of education that was then growing up in India under British Rule.

45

Gandhi could claim no such intellectual heritage in his businesslike Gujarat and Kathiawad. But thanks to the efficient means of communication established by the British, the stirrings of new life in other parts of India could not have failed to reach Gandhi imperceptibly. "The writings of Ram Mohan Roy, Devendranath Tagore, Rajendra Lal Mitra, in Bengal; those of Ranade, Vishnu Pundit, and others in Maharashtra, of Swami Dayananda (1824–1883, founder of the Arya Samaj), and Sir Syed Ahmed Khan in Upper India; of Madame Blavatsky and the other Theosophists in Madras, brought about a new awakening, which afterward received an even stronger impetus from the writings and speeches of Mrs. Annie Besant and Swami Vivekananda. This was on the religious and social side mainly, but its national character was unmistakable." [1] It was a day of new associations and societies, which sprang up throughout India, all aiming at the people's regeneration, national self-purification, and social uplift. Social reform movements had their apostles and energetic organizers, some aiming at the breakdown of caste rigidity, some espousing the cause of the untouchables, some working for the emancipation of women. The All-India National Congress was founded in 1885 as an effect of this new awakening.

Tagore (1861–1941) and Gandhi (1869–1948) grew up in such an invigorating and challenging atmosphere. But they were destined to go different ways. Tagore, as a poet and an aesthete, preferred the life of contemplation and became India's interpreter and ambassador of goodwill to the Western world; while Gandhi, as a "businessman" dedicated to God, and as a man of action, became India's trumpet voice, bearing the message of healing and reconciliation the while he offered non-violent battle to entrenched injustice both foreign and domestic.

Pandit Nehru's comments represent the best estimate of these two sons of Mother India: [2]

"Tagore and Gandhi have undoubtedly been the two outstanding and dominating figures of India in this first half of the twentieth century. It is instructive to compare and contrast them. No two persons could be so different from one another in their make-up or temperaments. Tagore, the aristocratic artist, turned democrat with proletarian sympathies, represented essentially the cultural tradition of India, the tradition of accepting life in the fullness thereof and going through it with song and dance. Gandhi, more a man of the people, almost the embodiment of the Indian peasant, represented the other ancient tradition of India, that of renunciation and asceticism. And yet Tagore was primarily the man of thought, Gandhi of concentrated and ceaseless activity. Both, in their different ways, had a world outlook, and both were at the same time wholly India. They seemed to represent different but harmonious aspects of India and to complement one another."

Each man held the other in high esteem. Both were working for India's regeneration, each in his own way. In the relations between these two men we see certain facets of Gandhi's personality, tender as a flower petal yet hard as steel.

When as a youth Tagore was singing patriotic songs for the uplift of his people, Gandhi was engaged in the meat-eating experiment with a view to making himself a patriot, a worthy match for the sturdy Englishman. When Tagore was engaged in the agitation against the partition of Bengal (1905–1911) and was preaching the gospel of *Swadeshi* (encouragement of home industries) and the whole of the non-cooperation movement in embryo, Gandhi was forging the weapons of non-violent warfare in far-off South Africa. Revolting against the violence that had crept into the Bengal agitation, Tagore retired from political life and took to the life of contemplation and of non-political service to his nation by establishing a school at Shantiniketan (the Abode of Peace). But there was always a touch of Gandhi's spirit in the poet; hence his school, from the very beginning, dedicated itself to rural uplift as well as to the formal training of students.

Gandhi paid Tagore the highest compliment he could by sending the Phoenix Ashram students to Shantiniketan in 1915 for temporary shelter—that is, until he was ready to establish his own Ashram and school in India.

Tagore's touching response to Gandhi's act is preserved for us in a letter written by the Poet: [3]

Dear Mr. Gandhi,

That you could think of my school as the right and the likely place where your Phoenix boys could take shelter when they are in India has given me real pleasure—and that pleasure has been greatly enhanced when I saw those dear boys in that place. We all feel that their influence will be of great value to our boys and I hope that they in their turn will gain something which will make their stay in Shanti-niketan fruitful. I write this letter to thank you for allowing your boys to become our boys as well and thus form a living link in the *sadhana* of both of our lives.

Very sincerely yours,
Rabindranath Tagore

That the tender-hearted Mahatma could be as hard as flint is best illustrated by the controversy between him and Tagore that took place soon after the inauguration of the non-violent non-cooperation movement (1920–1924). Gandhi's program called for a burning of foreign cloth, for the plying of the spinning wheel by the nation, for non-cooperation with the British system of education and with the British Raj as a whole. The movement disturbed Tagore; he looked upon it as a doctrine of negation and despair, as a doctrine of separatism, exclusiveness, and narrowness. In three forceful letters, appearing in *The Modern Review* of Calcutta, Tagore expressed his anxiety.

An able editorial, entitled "The Poet's Anxiety," in *Young India*, June 1, 1921, was Gandhi's rejoinder to the Poet: [4] "The Poet of Asia . . . is fast becoming the Poet of the World. Increasing prestige has brought to him increasing responsibility. His greatest service to India must be his poetic interpretation of India's message to the world. The Poet is therefore sincerely anxious that India should deliver no false or feeble message in her name. He is naturally jealous of his country's reputation. . . . No Indian can feel anything but pride in the Poet's exquisite jealousy of India's honor. . . . In all humility, I shall endeavor to answer the Poet's doubts."

The Poet's concern over the lot of the students who deserted government schools and had no other schools to go to, was met by the simple affirmation: "I have never been able to make a fetish of literary training. My experience has proved to my satisfaction that literary training by itself adds not an inch to one's moral height, and that character-building is independent of literary training. I am firmly of opinion that the government schools have unmanned us, rendered us helpless and Godless. . . . And if it was wrong to cooperate with the government in keeping us slaves, we were bound to begin with those institutions in which our association appeared to be most voluntary. . . ."

To the Poet's fear that non-cooperation might erect a Chinese wall between India and the West, Gandhi replied: "On the contrary, non-cooperation is intended to pave the way to real, honorable and voluntary cooperation based on mutual respect and trust. The present struggle is being waged against compulsory cooperation. . . ."

Concerning the so-called negative aspect of non-violent non-cooperation, Gandhi said: "We had lost the power of saying No. . . . This deliberate refusal to cooperate is like the necessary weeding process that the cultivator has to resort to before he sows. Weeding is as necessary to agriculture as sowing. . . . It is as necessary to reject untruth as it is to accept truth. . . . If India is ever to attain the Swaraj of the Poet's dream, she will do so only by non-violent non-cooperation. Let him deliver his message of peace to the world, and feel confident that India, through her non-cooperation, if she remains true to her pledge, will have exemplified his message. . . ."

This rejoinder failed to convince Tagore. He contributed to *The Modern Review* of October, 1921, a critique of the non-cooperation movement. This article of Tagore's, this "brilliant essay on the present movement" by "the Bard of Shantiniketan," as Gandhi put it, tried the Mahatma's patience. Any other leader, unschooled in patience, humility, and freedom from wrath, would have written a foolish and angry rejoinder. Instead, in an editorial entitled "The Great Sentinel" (*Young India,* October 13, 1921) Gandhi began by paying a compliment to the Poet: [5] "It [the article] is a series of word pictures which he alone can paint.

It is an eloquent protest against authority," against "slave mentality," against impatience. "The Poet tells us summarily to reject anything and everything that does not appeal to our reason or heart.
. . . His essay serves as a warning to us all who in our impatience
are betrayed into intolerance or even violence against those who
differ from us. I regard the Poet as a sentinel warning us against
the approach of enemies called Bigotry, Lethargy, Intolerance,
Ignorance, Inertia, and members of that brood."

Then rising to poetic heights matching those of Tagore himself, Gandhi said: "I do indeed ask the poet and the page to spin
the wheel as a sacrament. When there is war, the poet lays down
the lyre, the lawyer his law reports, the schoolboy his books. The
poet will sing the true note after the war is over, the lawyer will
have occasion to go to his law books when people have time to
fight among themselves. When a house is on fire, *all* the inmates
go out, and each one takes up a bucket to quench the fire. When
all about me are dying for want of food, the only occupation
permissible to me is to feed the hungry. It is my conviction that
India is a house on fire because its manhood is being daily
scorched; it is dying of hunger because it has no work to buy
food with. . . ."

The spinning wheel, argued Gandhi, would create work for
the hungry and would buy them food. Spinning thus became a
sacrament, an act of identification with the poor and with the
God of the poor (*Daridranarayana*). To quote Gandhi: "To a
people famishing and idle, the only acceptable form in which God
can dare appear is work and promise of food as wages. God created man to work for his food, and said that those who ate without work were thieves. Eighty per cent of India are compulsorily
thieves half the year. Is it any wonder if India has become one
vast prison? Hunger is the argument that is driving India to the
spinning wheel. The call of the spinning wheel is the noblest of
all—because it is the call of love. And love is Swaraj."

Tagore was irked by Gandhi's crusade for the burning of
foreign clothes. Said Gandhi: "I venture to suggest to the Poet
that the clothes I ask him to burn must be and are his. If they had
to his knowledge belonged to the poor or the ill-clad, he would

long ago have restored to the poor what was theirs." Would it not be better, Tagore asked in effect, to give these foreign-made clothes to the ill-clad instead of consigning them to the flames? "In burning my foreign clothes," said Gandhi, "I burn my shame. I must refuse to insult the naked by giving them clothes they do not need, instead of giving them work which they sorely need."

Categorically denying that either non-cooperation or Swadeshism was an exclusive doctrine, Gandhi said: "My modesty has prevented me from declaring from the house top that the message of non-cooperation, non-violence and Swadeshi is a message to the world." Tagore's alarm over the "exclusive" and "destructive" nature of the new-born nationalism was quieted with Gandhi's assertion: "Indian nationalism is not exclusive, nor aggressive, nor destructive. It is health-giving, religious and, therefore, humanitarian. India must learn to live before she can aspire to die for humanity. The mice which helplessly find themselves between the cat's teeth acquire no merit from enforced sacrifice."

"A drowning man cannot save others. In order to be fit to save others, we must try to save ourselves." Hence the program of non-violent non-cooperation for achieving India's freedom. Non-cooperation was not designed as a substitute for cooperation: it was designed as a substitute for violent warfare. "Our non-cooperation is neither with the English nor with the West. Our non-cooperation is with the system the English have established, with the material civilization and its attendant greed and exploitation of the weak."

As Gandhi rose to poetic heights at the beginning of the article, so did he display a lyric quality in its conclusion:

"True to his poetical instinct, the Poet lives for the morrow and would have us do likewise. He presents to our admiring gaze the beautiful picture of the birds early in the morning singing hymns of praise as they soar into the sky. These birds had their day's food and soared with rested wings in whose veins new blood had flowed during the previous night. But I have had the pain of watching birds who for want of strength could not be coaxed even into a flutter of their wings. The human bird under the

Indian sky gets up weaker than when he pretended to retire. For millions it is an eternal vigil or an eternal trance. It is an indescribably painful state which has to be experienced to be realized. I have found it impossible to soothe suffering patients with a song from Kabir. The hungry millions ask for one poem—invigorating food. They cannot be given it. They must earn it. And they can earn only by the sweat of their brow."

It was only in this controversy with Tagore that Gandhi betrayed impatience and resentment. In his editorial, "English Learning," *Young India,* June 1, 1921, Gandhi carried forward the argument with Tagore.[6] Having read Tagore's letter to the Manager of Shantiniketan, Gandhi said: "I am sorry to observe that the letter is written in anger and in ignorance of facts. The Poet was naturally incensed to find that certain students in London would not give a hearing to Mr. (W. W.) Pearson, one of the truest of Englishmen, and he became equally incensed to learn that I had told our women to stop English studies. The reasons for my advice, the Poet evidently inferred for himself.

"How much better it would have been if he had not imputed the rudeness of the students to non-cooperation, and had remembered that non-cooperators worship Andrews [an Englishman], honor Stokes [an American], and gave a respectful hearing to [a group of *notable Englishmen*] at Nagpur! . . . How much better it would have been if he had refused to allow the demon doubt to possess him for one moment as to the real and religious character of the present movement, and had believed that the movement was altering the meaning of old terms, nationalism and patriotism, and extending their scope.

"If he, with a poet's imagination, had seen that I was incapable of wishing to cramp the mind of the Indian women, and that I could not object to English learning as such, and recalled the fact that throughout my life I have fought for the fullest liberty for women, he would have been saved the injustice which he has done me and which, I know, he would never knowingly do to an avowed enemy."

Gandhi ended this heated editorial with a stern warning: "If he will be patient, he will find no cause for sorrow or shame for his countrymen. I respectfully warn him against mistaking its excrescences for the movement itself. It is as wrong to judge non-cooperation by the students' misconduct in London . . . as it would be to judge Englishmen by the Dyers or the O'Dwyers."

Ruffled as his temper seems to have been in this editorial, Gandhi redeemed the situation by stating two of his noblest conceptions. Defending his advice to the girls to give up the study of English, Gandhi said:

"I hope I am as great a believer in free air as the great Poet. I do not want my house to be walled in on all sides and my windows to be stuffed. I want the cultures of all the lands to be blown about my house as freely as possible. But I refuse to be blown off my feet by any."

Rebuking the poet for misreading the religious character of the movement, the Mahatma said:

"Mine is not a religion of the prison-house. It has room for the least among God's creation. But it is proof against insolence, pride of race, religion or color."

The upshot of this great controversy, perhaps needless in view of the inner harmony between Gandhi and Tagore, was that the poet was silenced and retired into his poet's corner in accordance with his own injunction: "If you can't march in step with your compatriots in the greatest crisis of their history, beware of saying they are in the wrong and you in the right! But give up your place in the ranks, and go back to the poet's corner and be prepared to meet with ridicule and public disgrace." [7] Retiring into his poet's corner, Tagore wrote in 1922 a memorable play *Mukta-Dhara* (The Waterfall) portraying the Gandhilike hero Dhananjaya Vairagi. Vairagi literally means "one who has renounced all personal possessions." The hero of the play assumed the leadership of his unarmed people in a no-tax campaign against the cruel exactions of the king. While Tagore was imaginatively creating *Satyagraha* on a mass scale, based on truth and non-violence, the flesh-and-blood hero was impelled by an inner compulsion to call off the Bardoli no-tax campaign in February, 1922—thanks to a violent outrage by his people in Chauri Chaura.

The controversy engendered bitterness on neither side; if

anything it made for deeper mutual respect. Thus on September 20, 1932, when he was to go on his "fast unto death" in prison against Prime Minister MacDonald's Communal Award, Gandhi remembered his great fellow-spirit and addressed a letter to "Dear Gurudev" (divine teacher), saying: "This is early morning three o'clock of Tuesday. I enter the fiery gate at noon. If you can bless the effort, I want it. You have been to me a true friend because you have been a candid friend, often speaking your thoughts aloud. If your heart approves the action, I want your blessing. It will sustain me. I hope I have made myself clear. My love." The letter was signed simply "M. K. Gandhi." But before the letter was dispatched, a telegram from Tagore was handed to Gandhi: "It is worth sacrificing precious life for the sake of India's unity and her social integrity. . . . Our sorrowing hearts will follow your sublime penance with reverence and love." Six days later the Poet was in Yeravada Prison, Poona, by Gandhi's bedside— just in time to receive the happy news that the British government had relented and Gandhi had won. Before the fast was broken, Tagore sang to Gandhi his beautiful song, a favorite of Gandhi's: "When the heart is dried up and parched, come with your shower of mercy."

The two met again in March, 1936, in Delhi and in March, 1938, in Calcutta. On both occasions Tagore was engaged in collecting funds for his Vishva-Bharati University at Shantini-ketan. Gandhi suggested that it was not fitting for the Poet at his age to go about begging for funds, that he wanted to know how much money was needed. On each occasion Gandhi promptly secured the needed money from his wealthy friends in the national movement. Then in February, 1940, "this great soul in a beggar's garb" went to see Tagore at Shantiniketan. This was their last meeting, and a very touching and beautiful one it was. A few months later the Poet was hovering between life and death. Gandhi sent his Secretary, Mahadev Desai, with a letter to Tagore. The Poet's hands shook with emotion and tears ran down his cheeks as he received Gandhi's letter.

Here were the two spiritual geniuses of India, each operating on his own plane, each enhancing the work of the other. The first meeting of these two outstanding sons of modern Mother India took place in 1915 when Gandhi, for the first time, reverently called Mahatma by Tagore, paid a visit to Shantiniketan in order to see the Poet and his Phoenix Ashramites who had received temporary shelter there. During that first visit Gandhi, true to his practice, suggested that students and teachers should do all the work and dispense with the services of hired help. When the proposition was broached to him by the students, the Poet exclaimed, "The experiment contains the key to *Swaraj*." Even though the experiment did not last long, to this day Shantiniketan observes March 10th every year as Gandhi Day. A holiday is given all the servants, and the students and teachers are required on that day to do all the chores, including the most menial ones.

The two met again during the Christmas week of 1917 when the Poet recited his "India's Prayer" at the opening session of the Calcutta Congress and Gandhi attended a performance of *The Post Office* at Tagore House.

In 1919–1920 the two vied with each other in showing their displeasure to the British Raj over the brutal Jallianwalla Bagh massacre in Amritsar. Tagore anticipated Gandhi's action and program of non-cooperation by a full year. On May 30, 1919, the Poet, renouncing his knighthood, wrote to the Viceroy: "The time has come when the badges of honor make our shame glaring in the incongruous context of humiliation, and I for my part wish to stand shorn of all special distinctions by the side of those of my countrymen who, for their so-called insignificance, are liable to suffer degradation not fit for human beings." On August 1, 1920, returning to the Viceroy the Kaiser-i-Hind medal bestowed on him for his services in the British-Boer War, and as a prelude to the launching of the non-violent non-cooperation movement, Gandhi wrote: "I can retain neither respect nor affection for a government which has been moving from wrong to wrong in order to defend its immorality."

Tagore was destined to be the immortal voice and Gandhi the invincible arm of the newborn nation. They were both at once nationalists and internationalists. Gandhi became an internationalist because he was first and foremost a nationalist (in political ideology). Tagore became a nationalist because he was first and foremost an internationalist. The end-result in both cases was the same though they traversed different paths. And who shall be arrogant enough to say that either one is the only correct path? It is possible, however, that in the world of tomorrow the Gandhi path is likely to be trodden by more people the world over than the Tagore path.

In spite of their divergence, how similar the two paths are is well brought out by Mr. K. R. Kripalani: [8]

"Though Gandhi had become the spearhead of Indian nationalism and Tagore was looked upon as the prophet of internationalism, Gandhi's mission of liberation embraces the entire humanity, and Tagore's love of his country was as deep-rooted and as intense as Gandhi's. 'I am wedded to India,' says Gandhi, 'because I believe absolutely that she has a mission for the world. My religion has no geographical limits. I have a living faith in it, which will transcend even my love for India herself.' Again: 'For me, patriotism is the same as humanity. I am patriotic because I am human and humane. My patriotism is not exclusive. I will not hurt England or Germany to serve India. . . . A patriot is so much less a patriot if he is a lukewarm humanitarian.' Tagore's patriotism needs no advocate. His songs have been on the lips of Bengal's martyrs being led to the gallows. He wanted the freedom of India not that she may shut herself up in her isolation nor that she should lord it over other nations, but that she may be in a position to offer to the world her best gifts and be able to accept from others the best they have to offer. He resented India's political subjection because to continue existence as 'the eternal rag-picker at other people's dust-bins' is the greatest shame. 'All humanity's greatest is mine. The infinite personality of man can only come from the magnificent harmony of all human races. My prayer is that India may represent the cooperation of all the peoples of the earth. For India unity is truth and division evil.' "

CHAPTER FIVE

GANDHI'S ECONOMICS

"I HAVE CLAIMED that I had been a socialist long before those I know in India avowed their creed. But my socialism was natural to me and not adopted from any books. It came out of my unshakable belief in non-violence. No man could be actively non-violent and not rise against social injustice, no matter where it occurred." Thus wrote Gandhi in his weekly paper *Harijan* of April 20, 1940.

Socialist literature has had no significant influence on Gandhi. His most intensive reading was done during his student days in London and his "barrister" days in South Africa. Gandhi's reading, for the most part, had been confined to character-building writings, religious, philosophical, and literary. The Bhagavad Gita and the Sermon on the Mount he had read in London. In South Africa he read Tolstoy, Ruskin, and Thoreau as well as the whole of the Bible, Commentaries on the Bible, Six Systems of Hindu Philosophy, and the history and tenets of world religions. In South Africa he translated into Gujarati Plato's *Apology,* or dialogue on the death of Socrates, and Ruskin's *Unto This Last.* It is not clear whether he first translated Thoreau's *Essay on Civil Disobedience* in South Africa or in India. Gandhi later translated the Bhagavad Gita from Sanskrit into Gujarati, with a commentary, under the title "The Yoga of Detachment." This book is now available in an English translation with notes by Gandhi's secretary, the late Mahadev Desai.

Gandhi's views on socialism changed with the passage of time. In the early days, he had a vague notion that socialists

57

wanted forcible redistribution of wealth: "I am no socialist, and I do not want to dispossess those who have got possessions. . . . I should then be departing from the rule of *Ahimsa*." [1] That was said in 1916. In 1940 he claimed to have been a socialist of long standing. During his last imprisonment in the Aga Khan's Palace, Poona, 1942–1944, out of courtesy to his socialist friends he decided to read Karl Marx's *Capital*. At the end of that herculean feat of endurance, he quietly remarked, "I think I could have written it better, assuming, of course, that I had the leisure for the study he has put in."

1. GANDHI'S PRIVATE UTOPIA

In order to understand Gandhi's economics it is necessary for us to distinguish between Gandhi the individual, with his private utopia, and Gandhi the citizen-leader, whose utopia must conform to social realities. Most writers dealing with this phase of Gandhi's thinking and activity have confused the two Gandhis, and, therefore, have failed to present a true picture of Gandhi's economics.

Gandhi the individual would feel thoroughly at home in the pre-social-contract order, postulated by Rousseau, wherein man lived by the noblest impulses of his nature, neither exploiting nor being exploited, neither impelled by lust for power nor submitting to the will of the tyrant, free from vice and corruption, unencumbered by possessions, eating freely of the bounty of nature, and "like the lilies of the field taking no thought of the morrow." The ideal way of life of Gandhi the individual could be best described in the words of the Chinese philosophers Laotze and Chuangtsu:

"In a small country with a few people let there be officers over tens and hundreds, but not in order to exercise power. Let the people be not afraid of death, nor desire to move to a distance. Then even though there be ships and carriages, they will have no occasion to use them; even though there be armor and weapons, they will have no necessity to wear them. The people can return to the knotted cords for the records; they can delight in their food, be content with their dwellings, and rejoice in their customs.

Neighboring countries may look at one another; they may be so close that their cocks and dogs may be mutually heard; but the people may grow old and die before they visit one another" (Laotze).[2]

"And so in the days when instincts prevailed, men moved quietly and gazed steadily. At that time there were no roads over mountains, nor boats, nor bridges over water. All things were produced, each for its own sphere. Birds and beasts multiplied; trees and shrubs grew up. The former might be led by the hand; you could climb up and peep into the raven's nest. For then men dwelt with birds and beasts, and all creation was one . . ." (Chuangtsu).[3]

The private utopia of Gandhi would be an idyllic existence on the Himalayan heights, perhaps by himself, perhaps with a few others of like mind; an existence in which he could live in harmony with nature, labor for himself a few hours, and commune with his inner self and with God. There would be no need to minister to others since none would need ministration.

In a grand gesture of living his phantasy as a reality, the Mahatma did actually establish a solitary abode in the open countryside near Wardha, with the hope of "living and working there in solitude" (1936). A single mud hut was built. Dr. John R. Mott interviewed Gandhi there in 1937. Village reconstruction workers would visit Gandhi there from time to time. Soon the sick and the infirm began to come in. Other cottages had to be built. A dispensary was established. A barn had to be built to accommodate cows. Dairy workers were needed, and new cottages went up. Thus, ruefully commented Gandhi, "In spite of myself, the place has developed into an Ashram without any rules and regulations. It is growing and new huts are springing up. Today it has become a hospital. In jest I have called it a 'Home for the Invalids.' . . . I have even likened it to a Lunatic Asylum. . . ."[4]

This last Ashram established by Gandhi, the Sevagram Ashram, illustrates the story of the Hindu recluse all over again. He lived in solitude the better to perform his *sadhana* or meditation. A mouse began to distract his attention. He decided to get a cat in order to chase the mouse away. The cat needed milk, and he bought a cow. It soon appeared that if he was to devote himself to meditation, he had to have someone to take care of the cow. And so on and so forth.

Gandhi, the citizen-leader, did not ever attempt, nor even think of attempting, to make society over into his image. He had already come to the conclusion that he could find neither God nor his true self apart from humanity. His private utopia, therefore, has no relevance in a discussion of Gandhi's economics.

2. AN OUTLINE OF GANDHI'S ECONOMICS

What, then, is the outline of Gandhi's public view of economics?

First, from Ruskin he had learned the heterodox economic doctrine that the wealth of a nation consisted in its people, not in its production and consumption goods (1904).

Second, from Sir Daniel Hamilton, an able financier with interests in India, he learned: "That India does not need to look to the gold standard or to the silver standard or to any metallic standard; [that] India has a metal all its own, and he says that that consists in her countless units of labor . . . since we have all the labor, we do not want to fall back upon any foreign capital. . . . We would be able to produce those things that the world would voluntarily and willingly take from us"[5] (1931). Here we have the labor theory of value expounded by Adam Smith, Ricardo, and Marx.

Third, his experiments with truth and non-violence led him to believe in the doctrines of non-thieving and non-possession. In lieu of the multiplicity of wants, which is the cornerstone of modern economics, Marxist as well as orthodox, Gandhi counselled a renunciation of wants as the true criterion of civilization. "A multiplicity of hospitals," he said, "is no test of civilization; it is rather a symptom of decay."[6] Just as he advocated prevention of disease by proper healthful living, so he advocated a renunciation of wants as a cure for the multiplying problems of the disease called modern civilization (1909). As Jawaharlal Nehru neatly put it: "In an acquisitive society madly searching for new gadgets and new luxuries, he takes to his loin-cloth and his mud-hut." [7]

Fourth, in the economy of India, the farmer, perforce rendered idle for six months in the year, used formerly to supplement his income from agriculture with the products of cottage industry—principally spinning and weaving. "The cottage industry, so vital for India's existence, has been ruined by incredibly heartless and inhuman processes as described by English witnesses." Further, "the miserable comfort [of town-dwellers] represents the brokerage they get for the work they do for the foreign exploiter; the profits and the brokerage are sucked from the masses." The British system of administration in India was "carried on for this exploitation of the masses. No sophistry, no jugglery in figures, can explain away the evidence the skeletons in many villages present to the naked eye" [8] (1922). Here we have practically Marx's thesis, without the Marxian jargon, that national capitalism (British in this case) tended to develop into finance capitalism and imperialism, to subjugate and exploit the colonial masses, and that the bourgeoisie, the town-dwellers, took the side of capitalism against the exploited masses.

Fifth, to be self-respecting and efficient, the worker must own his own tools of production, namely, the spinning wheel and the handloom, and the farmer must own the farm he tills.

These basic assumptions of Gandhi's economics came into a head-on collision with the infant industrialism of India, ushered into being, first, by British capitalists and, later, by Hindese capitalists. Gandhi's response has been misunderstood. He has been maligned as advocating a throwback to primitive economy, a retreat from the industrial-urban complex. There is no truth in such a distorted interpretation.

Time and again Gandhi said, "I am not opposed to machine *qua* machine"; he himself was adept at the use of the spinning wheel—a machine! What he objected to were the uses to which large-scale machinery was put: exploitation of human beings, concentration of power and riches in the hands of the few, technological unemployment, and consequent starvation of those displaced by the machine.

Economists would accept the first two indictments of the machine, at least so far as past experience is concerned, but would quarrel with Gandhi's third count of indictment. Technological unemployment is at best a temporary phenomenon; indeed, any new technological invention may provide employment for millions while temporarily displacing hundreds. For instance, hundreds of hansom cab drivers were thrown out of employment by the appearance of the automobile; but the automobile industry provided new employment to millions in various phases of industry, and in taxicab service. There is logic in the economist's argument, but Gandhi was concerned with human values. The technologically displaced may appear as a statistical figure to the economist; to Gandhi they appeared as human beings with mouths to feed, with joys and sorrows, with wives and children who would suffer from their unemployment. Furthermore, in the specific conditions of India, the primary problem was, and is, employment of its teeming millions leading to production; not production as a result of employment of labor and use of machinery.

Gandhi stated his point neatly: "I have no objection if all things required by my country could be produced with the labor of 30,000 instead of that of 30,000,000. But those 30,000,000 must not be rendered idle or unemployed." [9] That the ultimate test of the validity of mass production must be general well-being is brought out by Gandhi in the following statement: "My object is not to destroy the machine. . . . I welcome the machine that lightens the burden of millions of men living in cottages and reduces man's labor. . . . If we could have electricity in every village home, I should not mind villagers plying their implements and tools with electricity." [10]

In other words, Gandhi would have no machine in his private utopia; but in the world of reality he would tame the machine in the interest of the masses. That is hardly a throwback to primitivism!

Taming the machine is not a one-man job; it requires the collective efforts of hundreds of members of society. And since he had no time to spare for such a titanic movement, Gandhi was content to lay down his general principles regarding the limits and possibilities of large-scale machinery in terms of human welfare—in terms of human weal-th. He would devote his own active energies to the rejuvenation of village life, to the rehabilitation of village industries, enkindling among village folk the "powers of love, of joy, and of admiration," and transforming this exploited, wretched humanity—85 per cent of India's population—into "noble and happy human beings." And since this activity fitted in with his temperamental and theoretical belief in the validity of decentralization, the Mahatma in his latter days devoted himself wholeheartedly to rural uplift, and organized the Village Industries and Reconstruction Association.

Our "Point Four" program will be effective in India—or anywhere else in the Orient, for that matter—only if we keep before us Gandhi's clear-cut analysis of the economic scene, and seek to help in the rejuvenation of village life. What India needs is not large-scale machinery—excepting hydroelectric projects—but technical know-how applied to transform the countryside into farms and gardens and orchards worked by "noble and happy human beings."

Devoted as he was to decentralization and village reconstruction, Gandhi could not wish out of existence the ubiquitous machine. A retreat from the machine age seemed out of the question. Had there been no railroads, there would have been no hardships for third-class passengers. But since the railroads did exist, Gandhi saw his duty in terms of a struggle to ameliorate the lot of third-class passengers. And since industrialism is bound up with the emergence of the class of employers and the class of employees—one endowed with power and riches, the other helpless and dependent—it became Gandhi's duty to help the employees, to show them the power of non-violent organization, to improve their conditions.

3. GANDHI'S MAGNA CHARTA FOR LABOR

Both in South Africa and in India Gandhi had shown his interest in the well-being of the worker in transport, factory, mine, and plantation. But his first entry into the labor movement of

India dates back to February, 1918. The occasion was a demand for a wage increase by the weavers employed in the textile mills of Ahmedabad. The workers were restless and there was danger of strike, lockout, and violence. Before jumping into the fray, Gandhi wanted to satisfy himself whether there was justice in the workers' demands. To that end, he had an investigation made of the living conditions of the workers in Ahmedabad, and their budgets studied—the first such piece of field work and survey in India. Once convinced of the justice of the workers' demands, Gandhi opened negotiations with the employers, and "strained every nerve to obtain a peaceful settlement. The millowners would not listen. His offer to submit the dispute to arbitration was rejected. The millowners could not brook the interference of any outsider." [11] Whereupon Gandhi proceeded to launch his non-violent struggle for "an equal voice for the workers in the determination of their terms of employment." [12] After a course of preliminary training in non-violence, Gandhi asked the workers to take a pledge of abstention from work till either their proffered terms were accepted or the demand for wage increase was arbitrated. Gandhi kept in constant touch with the strikers, "addressed mass meetings, and issued pamphlets daily. Every day the workers paraded the streets in peaceful procession." [13]

Let the rest of the story be told in his own words by Mr. Nanda, intimately associated with Gandhi and with the Ahmedabad Textile Labor Association ever since its inception: [14]

"In about three weeks, demoralization set in among the workers on strike. Some of them began to waver. They said they had no food for themselves and their families. On the morning of March 12, 1918, facing a meeting of the strikers, Gandhiji made an unexpected announcement. He declared he would himself touch no food till the workers' pledge was redeemed. This was Gandhiji's first fast on a public issue in India. It electrified the workers and restored their morale. This was its sole aim. The millowners on their side were touched. They shed their complacency and bestirred themselves to find a way out. At the end of three days, arbitration was agreed to and Gandhiji broke his fast. The principle and procedure of arbitration which have played so large a part in making the Textile Labor Association what it is today were thus introduced in the industrial relations in this country for the first time.

"On February 25, 1920, Gandhiji inaugurated the first regular union of the workers in the textile industry. In May he asked the employers to reduce the hours of work from twelve to ten and make a substantial addition to the wages of the operatives. Agreement not having been reached between the arbitrators either regarding the terms of the award or the choice of the umpire, Gandhiji took the workers out on a strike which lasted ten days. Work was resumed when a joint award was issued introducing a ten-hour day in the industry and effecting an increase in wages ranging from 25 per cent to 62½ per cent for different occupations. To the workers Gandhiji declared on this occasion that it was not their triumph but the triumph of justice and hence a victory for both the sides."

A Charter for Labor, according to Gandhi, ought to include the following ten points: [15]

1. Labor is entitled to an equal voice in the determination of its conditions of employment. In case of disagreement, the decision of an impartial tribunal should prevail.

2. Labor has the right to a share in the administration and control of the industry.

3. The remuneration of all engaged in the industry should be as nearly equal as possible.

4. The standard living wage of a male adult should be sufficient to provide for health and efficiency of the entire family, and a few extra items.

5. Conditions of work should not prove fatiguing to workers, provision being made for recreation, etc.

6. Workers' health must be safeguarded.

7. Employers should provide for "the creature comforts" of workers during employment, "decent accommodation for rest and refreshment, sufficient water and satisfactory sanitary facilities."

8. Employers must provide suitable housing to workers without impairing their freedom in any way.

9. The workers have an inalienable right to organize, to form unions, and to bargain collectively.

10. In case of refusal to arbitrate, or failure or undue delay in implementing an award, the workers have an unrestricted right to strike.

The constitution of the Ahmedabad Textile Labor Association (1920) specifically emphasizes reliance strictly on truth and non-violence—a provision which was already an integral part of Gandhi's political movement.

While he was willing to speak for the rights of labor, Gandhi was more concerned with duties than with rights—the duties of employees to employers, the duties of employers to employees. The employers, having greater power and riches, he felt, had greater and higher obligations than the employees; they must act as trustees. Gandhi believed that if the capitalist failed properly to discharge his duties as a trustee, then capitalism was doomed.

4. Gandhism Versus Marxism

What are the differences between Gandhism and Marxism, as represented by socialism and communism? Gandhi, as well as the socialists and the communists, all accept the labor theory of value; implicit in Gandhi's thinking would be the theory of surplus value, first propounded by Karl Marx. Like Marxists, Gandhi believed that labor was exploited by capital. Unlike Marx, who postulated an inevitable class conflict, Gandhi believed that the antagonistic interests of labor and capital could be and must be harmonized by an equal partnership between employer and employee. Gandhi also believed that "key industries," public utilities in our terminology, employing capital beyond the reach of ordinary citizens, must be owned and operated by the State in the interest of all the citizens; but he clearly visualized the ownership of farms by farmers, of small-scale industries by individuals, partnerships, cooperatives, or corporations; and the ownership of large-scale industries other than public utilities by corporations or cooperatives on the basis of a partnership between capital and labor.

If the essence of socialism be complete collectivism and nationalization of the means of production, distribution, and exchange, then Gandhi was not a socialist. If the abolition of private property be the crux of socialism, then Gandhi was not a socialist. But if socialism be equated with sympathy and solidarity with the exploited masses, with a passion and striving for social justice, with an economic arrangement conducive to the free development of human personality, with a peaceful international society free from exploitation, then certainly Gandhi was a socialist, as pointed out by M. R. Masani, himself a socialist and author of *Our India*. Indeed this was precisely the connotation of the term socialism before the founders of so-called "scientific socialism," Marx and Engels, gave it the Marxist meaning. Gandhi would retrieve socialism from the clutches of Marxism.

Let us give Marx the benefit of the doubt, and assume he meant by the term socialism social good and by communism the common good; i.e., the good of society as a whole. With such a goal there can be no quarrel; it was precisely Gandhi's goal. But where Marx erred was in conceiving society primarily as composed of two clashing classes. Society is a complex of groups, millions of groups large and small, each intent on pursuing its own interest or set of interests. To be sure, the social process does involve competition and conflict, but it also involves socialization of the newborn, cooperation, accommodation, assimilation, social control, social change.

Having simplified society and the social process into interplay between two conflicting classes, it was inevitable that Marx should set up as the goal of his economic system a classless society. However, on both theoretical and practical grounds, the existence of a classless society is an impossibility. Every attempt to submerge classes leads to the emergence of a mass society, resting upon totalitarian dictatorship. In Soviet Russia's efforts to achieve a classless society, we witness rule by the elite class on the one hand and mass-mindedness at the bottom of the layer on the other. Democracy, to be meaningful, must permit the emergence, organization, and functioning of voluntary groups and associations; it must set forth rules for the minimization of conflict between classes. There is a great deal of truth in Marx's assertion of the existence of the class struggle in society, in the labor theory of value, and in the theory of surplus value. The economic interpretation of history, likewise, has an important element of truth; but as an all-sufficient explanation for human behavior, it is misleading, false, and mischievous.

Furthermore, Marx underrated the dynamic of national loyalty. His prediction that the social revolution would take place first in highly industrialized countries has been proved to be wrong; it took place in Russia, an industrially underdeveloped country. He was equally wrong in his categorical assumption that with advance in technology and increase in production, the workers' share of the national income would steadily diminish: as a matter of fact, the worker in the United States of America today enjoys luxuries such as were unavailable to royalty in Marx's day. Again, the business corporation in America with its millions of stockholders actually tends to establish partnership between capital and labor. Finally, though we grant there is some amount of distributive injustice under capitalism, the answer may be sought, in a democratic society, not in bullets but in ballots.

Socialists and communists alike accept the Marxian analysis of the social process. Gandhi would totally reject it. While Marx spoke of history, past and present, as being a record of conflict between two contending parties, Gandhi said: "History is a record of the interruptions in the even working of the force of love or of the soul"; which is to say, history as it is written, not "as it happened," records interruptions in cooperation and non-violence.[16] But the major portion of human existence is, for Gandhi, compounded not of conflicts but of harmony. The class conflict between employers and employees was an aberration and had to be settled by non-violent methods.

While Gandhi parts company both from socalists and communists in regard to certain basic assumptions, methods, and goals, the socialists and communists part company from each other on the score of methods alone. The socialist, accepting the Marxian analysis, would bring about the collectivist society by constitutional procedures within a democratic framework, by the use of the ballot box; the communist, on the other hand, would bring about the collectivist society by brute force, by capture of power, by capturing the State machinery.

Having captured power by brute force, the communist would maintain his power by brute force, by imposing a dictatorship of the proletariat, by using the State as a class tool to expropriate and liquidate the propertied classes. When the transitional period is over, say the Marxist-communists, the bourgeois class will have been liquidated, the classless society will emerge, and the State will "wither away." The experience of the Soviet Union suggests that the transitional stage constantly projects farther and farther into the future; that a new elite class takes the place of the bourgeoisie and dictates to the proletariat; that the Soviet State becomes more ubiquitous with its secret service agents and more centralized with bureaucracy than the bourgeois tsarist State ever was!

Furthermore, it was Marx's thesis that patriotism, fatherland, loyalty to the State, and religion were myths created by the bourgeoisie for the exploitation of the masses; "the working men," he said, "have no country"; the workers of the world have one common interest, namely, to end exploitation. Let us see how this aspect of the Marxian thesis is borne out by concrete experience. The Soviet Government of Russia, which had come into power on the premise of the solidarity of the workers of the world, is today more nationalistic, chauvinistic, and imperialistic, than capitalist America. The tables have been turned. The Soviet Government is more capitalistically motivated than the bourgeois democracy of America. And the American Government is more socialistically oriented than the so-called "workers' government" of Russia. America is not demanding heavy reparations from the workers of defeated Germany; it is the workers' government of the Soviet Union which does. Stalin is giving the lie to Marx's assertion that "the working men have no country." The German workingmen have Germany as their country, to be exploited by the Russian workingmen who have Russia as their country!

While the empirical experience of the working of Marxism and communism in the Soviet Union and elsewhere has been dis-

astrous to the well-being of the masses, Gandhi's quarrel with it
would be on yet another plane. To begin with, the communist
system is a totalitarian dictatorship and, therefore, a positive evil,
worse than the British Raj was. Furthermore, communism is a
negation of the moral and spiritual values held in high esteem by
mankind through the ages. For instance, though it is attested by
the universal experience of mankind that truth is cherished as a
virtue for its own sake and as a guide to human conduct in interpersonal relations, the communists exalt lying and falsehood as
virtues. Second, non-violence has been held as a virtue by mankind through the ages, even though we may have strayed into the
path of violence; yet the communists glorify violence as a means
of seizing and maintaining power. Third, honor in interpersonal
relations has been exalted by the universal experience of mankind,
but the communists preach and practise dishonor as a virtue—
spying upon fellow men, infiltration or "boring from within."
Fourth, respect for the dignity of the individual and the worth of
human personality are inculcated by every authentic religion; but
the secular religion of communism makes of the human being a
predetermined automaton, a cog in the machine of the State,
bereft of freedom of will and freedom of choice. Fifth and last,
victimized though it might have been, now and then, by the lust
for material might, mankind has ever held aloft the overriding
power of spiritual vision and power; the communists make a
fetish of materialism, deriving their fanatical ideology from a
materialistic or economic interpretation of history.

Contrast the Marxist dialectics and the Stalinist performance with Gandhi's vision of the society of a free India (1931) to
be achieved by non-violence: [17]

"I shall strive for a constitution which shall release India
from all thraldom and patronage and give her, if need be, the
right to err. I shall work for an India in which the poorest shall
feel that it is their country, in whose making they have an effective
voice; an India in which there shall be no high class and no low
class of people; an India in which all communities shall live in
perfect harmony. There can be no room in such an India for
the curse of untouchability, or the curse of intoxicating drinks or

drugs. Women shall enjoy equal rights with men. Since we shall be at peace with all the rest of the world, neither exploiting nor being exploited, we should have the smallest army imaginable. All interests not in conflict with the interests of the dumb [i.e., inarticulate—H. T. M.] millions will be scrupulously respected whether foreign or indigenous. Personally I hate distinction between foreign and indigenous. This is the India of my dreams for which I shall struggle at the next Round Table. . . ."

His vision of a free India within the bounds of practical politics was realized on August 15, 1947. But Gandhi had his ideal dreams as well. In 1939 he said: "Sometimes a man lives in his daydreams. I live in mine, and picture the world as full of good human beings—not goody-goody human beings. In the socialist's language, there will be a new structure of society, a new order of things. I also am aspiring after a new order of things that will astonish the world." [18] The outlines of this new structure were not left to us by Mahatma Gandhi; but on the basis of our discussion, it should not be difficult to visualize Gandhi's ideal structure of society.

To exorcise the demon of misunderstanding once and for all, let me repeat: Gandhi had his private utopia; he had his public utopia, i.e., an ideal order for the public at large; but he actually worked for the fulfillment of his vision of a free India—a vision which was well within the scope of practical politics and economic realities.

5. A FOOTNOTE TO GANDHI'S ECONOMICS

Gandhi's basic economic tenets are being implemented by Free India in unexpected and extraordinary ways. First, the Government of India has enacted progressive social legislation in behalf of industrial workers. Second, the Trade Union movement is flourishing, and promoting the well-being of workers. Third, legislation, bringing relief to debt-ridden peasantry, is in operation in some of the states of the Republic of India. Fourth, with American technical aid, the Government of India has been building hydro-electric works which will help realize Gandhi's dream

of "having electricity in every village home." Fifth and most spec-
tacular, one of Gandhi's followers, Vinoba Bhavé, has been engaged in realizing two of Gandhi's basic economic principles in
the strictly Gandhi fashion. We have pointed out that Gandhi
believed (1) in the right of farmers to own farms and (2) in the
role of the wealthy as trustees. These two points are being realized
simultaneously by Mr. Bhavé in a very unorthodox fashion.

In the spring of 1951, Vinoba Bhavé undertook a journey
on foot in a communist-infested region of Hyderabad State. On
June 9, 1951, the Hyderabad Government Information Bureau
released the following news item:

"Acharya (*Teacher-Priest*) Vinoba Bhavé, who has been
touring Telangana on foot since April 6, 1951, concluded his
tour at Mancherial on June 6, 1951. During his historic tour, he
encamped at 51 villages, studied the conditions of about 200 villages and addressed more than two *lakhs* (200,000) persons.
'*Sarvodaya* is a better alternative to communism,' he said wherever
he went.

"Acharya Vinoba Bhavé, in the course of his tour, settled
more than 500 village disputes. They were referred to him by the
parties themselves. Acharyaji has received about 9,000 acres of
land for distribution among the landless." (*By exact count, the
number of acres donated was 12,000. H.T.M.*)

A Land-Gifts Mission Committee (*Bhu-Dan-Yajna Samiti,*
sometimes also called *Bhumi-Dan-Yajna Samiti*), organized by
Bhavé before his departure from the region, has been functioning
and turning over acres of donated land to land-hungry peasants.
The resolution passed by the Hyderabad Congress Committee on
June 15, 1951, extolling Vinoba Bhavé's work, underscores the
meaning of this new move as a factor in the reconstruction of
India's agrarian economy:

"This session of the All-Hyderabad Congress Committee
expresses its earnest gratitude to Poojya (*Revered*) Vinoba
Bhavé for the valuable services rendered by him in his walking
tour in Telangana and for effectively using the weapon of love
and non-violence in solving agrarian problems as against the one
based on hatred and violence preached and practised by commu-

nists to the detriment of the country; and (it) appeals to the people of Hyderabad and particularly the Congress workers to continue the pious work of *bhu-dan* (land-gift) started by him."

Since that memorable tour in the spring of 1951, the idea of the Land-Gift Mission spread all over India. Everywhere, in every state, Vinoba would make a pilgrimage on foot and ask for land-gifts. That landless and land-hungry farmers would be willing to accept land is understandable; but that there should be landlords by the thousands willing to give away part of their land as a gift is beyond the understanding of Western man. Yet, a situation very similar to this must have been in Gandhi's mind when he spoke of riches as being a trust and the rich man as a trustee.

A year after the start of the movement, Vinoba reviewed the results of his Land-Gift Mission in a speech before the Sarvodaya Conference, on April 13, 1952.[19] Incidentally, *Sarvodaya,* i.e., *Welfare of All,* was Gandhi's rendition into Gujarati of Ruskin's *Unto This Last.* The Sarvodaya Movement is carried on by Gandhi's intimate associates and disciples in order to promote the *constructive program* Gandhi had launched. In this review, Vinoba stressed the Gandhi point of view that God's grace and self-help on the part of the people are more important than legislation:

"The powers of the indwelling Spirit are immeasurable and unlimited. . . . We have seen that without the pressure of law people have parted with their lands. When I explain to them that like air, water, light, etc., land is also a gift of God and all sons of the soil have an equal right to it, they willingly respond to my appeal and donate lands. . . . One Zamindar (*landlord*) donated 500 out of his 1900 acres, saying that they were three brothers, and now I was the fourth. Similarly, another accepted me as his third brother and gifted two acres from his six. . . . Hence I proceed with my work in the faith that the Spirit is present in all men, and that there is no limit to His powers. . . ."

Should there be agitation for legislation making land-gift mandatory for all big landlords? To that question, Vinoba replied: "Let it be left to the legislators. We must follow our own method of doing it. Maybe all land might get distributed among the landless through the Land-Gifts Movement, and there might not at all remain any occasion for legislation. But if human will fails to become strong and successful enough to solve the land problem and if it becomes necessary to resort to legislation, our achievement will pave the way for legislation. That is to say, our achievement will either make legislation unnecessary or create an atmosphere for its easy passage."

In asking land for the landless, Vinoba does not beg alms: "I ask for the land as a right of the poor." If a big landlord were to make a token offering, Vinoba would graciously refuse the gift: "I desire to humiliate neither the poor nor the rich . . . To cite an incident: A landlord owning 300 acres came and offered me an acre. I declined to accept the gift. On my explaining to him my point of view, he unreservedly raised his donation to 30 acres. It took hardly two minutes to persuade him. . . . About ten thousand persons have so far donated lands in this way. Some of these donations are indeed examples of such nobleness of mind that I shall carry their sacred memory throughout my life."

The Land-Gifts Movement, as part of Sarvodaya, is designed to "stave off a violent revolution" and to correct an iniquitous social situation by non-violent methods, in the spirit of Mahatma Gandhi. The movement serves a double purpose. On the one hand, it affords the landlord an opportunity to discharge his duty as a trustee; on the other hand, it redeems the landless peasant who will now put his heart and soul into the good earth newly acquired as his very own. The Sarvodaya Movement and its noblest exemplar, Vinoba Bhavé, are translating into reality Gandhi's economic thoeries, principles and beliefs. In the perspective of history, this Sarvodaya work of Vinoba, implementing Gandhi's economic teachings, will loom larger than the planning programs of the Government of India. This magnificent spectacle of Gandhi's economics in action is unparalleled even in the history of India!

CHAPTER SIX

GANDHI'S PEDAGOGY

A LL GREAT men are founders of schools, either in the sense of having a following, i.e., a body of persons banded together formally or informally around the great man's teaching, or in the sense of establishing a center of learning. Buddha and Jesus, Confucius and Laotze were founders of schools in the first sense. Socrates with his "school" in the market-place of Athens, Plato with his Academy, Aristotle with his peripatetic "school" were all founders of schools in both senses of the term. In recent times Pestalozzi and Montessori, Gandhi and Tagore have been founders of schools in both senses. The centers of learning founded by them and the following they secured are characteristically unique and pedagogically enriching; each of them was moved by profound concern for the well-being of the underprivileged. Perhaps here we have a formula for the making of a great teacher, a great educator, a great man—profound concern for the well-being of the underprivileged.

For a sound pedagogy we must go not to professors of education nor to teachers but to great leaders of mankind, such as Buddha and Jesus; to great leaders of nations, such as Mahatma Gandhi of India in our day; to great leaders of small groups, such as Froebel, Pestalozzi, and Montessori.

Pestalozzi was an effective educator because he was a great man, the mark of his greatness being sensitivity to the conditions of the village folk of Switzerland and his pioneer work in their behalf. Montessori is an effective educator because she is a great woman, the distinguishing trait of her greatness being sensitivity to the conditions of subnormal children in Italy and her pioneer work in their behalf. Gandhi was an effective educator because he was a great man, and one of the marks of his greatness was a sensitivity to the plight of the underprivileged children of the "untouchables."

Gandhi had been drawn to education, to schooling in the formal sense, during his South African days (1893–1914). At Phoenix Ashram and at Tolstoy Farm, it fell to his lot to impart education to young children committed to his care. These early experiences left their abiding impress upon Gandhi throughout his life, but his real grappling with the problems of education did not come about until after 1932 when he launched the crusade for the abolition of untouchability.

The call of systematic pedagogy, as of village reconstruction, came rather late in Gandhi's life. His achievements in other fields of activity were so overwhelming that mankind has paid scant attention to the philosophy and techniques of education worked out by the Mahatma. All too often has the world heard of Mahatma Gandhi as saint or statesman. A modern Isaiah, he is presented to us as a prophet calling upon his people—and the people of the world—to tread the path of righteousness. We have had pictures of the holy man, scantily dressed, moving up and down the plains of Hindustan preaching the gospel of simplicity and dedication, plying the symbolic spinning wheel, releasing from age-old bondage the outcaste and the oppressed. There is conjured up before our mind's eye the vision of a guileless saint matching his wits with the British statesmen at the Round Table Conference in London. The Mahatma, as the world is rightly led to believe, had no truck with equivocation which to him was a species of violence; and yet his straightforward, non-violent technique confounded the most astute British diplomatists. In other words, we have always thought of Gandhi as a holy saint who in some marvelous manner possessed the qualities of a rare statesman.

1. Psychologist and Theorist

Had Gandhi been born in a free country, he would most probably have devoted his entire energies to the amelioration of the underprivileged and to the education of the people. I shall cite a few instances to illustrate Gandhi's skill as a child psychologist and educationist.[1]

In London at Kingsley Hall Gandhi once met with some of the children of the neighborhood. His technique was simple and effective. He told the English children about Hindese children. He spoke of the common interests that children all over the world have, such as learning, playing, and having a good time. The conversation led to possibilities of quarrels among playmates. Gandhi asked, "How many of you hit your opponent when you felt your rights were denied or you were called names?" One boy triumphantly raised his hand. The others were meekly expectant. Gandhi patted the boy on the back and said, "Bravo! I see you are an honest boy." Continuing, he said: "You should stand up for your rights, but you can convince your opponent much better by arguing with him, by reasoning with him, by showing him the wrong he has done. The way of love is better than the way of fighting." The very spirit of goodness and friendliness filled the room as Gandhi and the children were talking. To the children of the East End of London he was not a Mahatma, nor an arch-rebel against England, but Uncle Gandhi.

A meeting between Madame Montessori and Gandhi in England brought two lovers of children face to face. Mme. Montessori spoke no English, but her Latin ardor and facial expressions were more eloquent than the translations by her secretary. At the reception given him by the Montessori Training School, the Mahatma made a gracious reply to the praise accorded him, and added some neat observations on child psychology:

"Madame, you have overwhelmed me with your words. It is perfectly true, I must admit in all humility, that, however indifferently it may be, I endeavor to represent Love in every fiber of my being. I am impatient to realize the presence of my Maker who to me embodies Truth, and in the early part of my career I discovered that if I was to realize the Truth I must obey, even at the cost of my life, the Law of Love. And having been blessed with children, I discovered that the Law of Love could best be understood and learned through little children. Were it not for us, their ignorant poor parents, our children would be perfectly innocent. I believe implicitly that the child is not born mischievous in the bad sense of the term. If parents behave themselves while the child is growing, the child will instinctively obey the Law of Truth and the Law of Love. . . .

"As I was watching those beautiful rhythmic movements of the children, my whole heart went out to the millions of children of the semi-starved villages of India. . . .

"Believe me, from my experience of hundreds—I was going to say thousands—of children, I know that they have perhaps a finer sense of honor than you and I have. The greatest lessons in life, if we would but stoop and humble ourselves, we would learn not from grown-up learned men but from the so-called ignorant children. Jesus never uttered a loftier or a grander truth than when he said that 'wisdom cometh out of the mouths of babes.' I believe it. I have noticed in my own experience that if we approached babes in humility and in innocence we would learn wisdom from them. . . ."

In 1935 the Mahatma made an important statement regarding the technique of educating children. In the anti-untouchability campaign attention was being focused upon the education of the children of Harijans (i.e., God's children, the new name given by Gandhi to untouchables) and upon adult education among Harijans. Warning against slavish imitation of the modes and methods of present-day schools, Gandhi said: [2]

"We have to recognize that we get Harijan children with great difficulty to attend any school at all. We can not expect any degree of regularity in them and, thanks to our past criminal neglect, they are so unkempt that we have, in the beginning stages, to handle them in a manner wholly different from the ordinary."

Then the Mahatma went on to enunciate certain fundamental principles of elementary teaching. They are so profound and so well put that I reproduce the statement verbatim:

"On first admission their [the children's] bodies have to be minutely examined and thoroughly cleaned. Their clothes might have to be cleaned and patched. The first daily lesson, therefore, will for some time consist of applied hygiene and sanitation and simple needle-work.

"I should use no books probably for the whole of the first year. I should talk to them about things with which they are familiar and, doing so, correct their pronunciation and grammar and teach them new words. I should note all the new words they may learn from day to day so as to enable me to use them frequently till they have them fixed in their minds regularly.

"The teacher will not give discourses but adopt the conversational method. Through conversations he will give his pupils progressive instruction in history, geography and arithmetic. History will begin with that of our own times, and then, too, of events and of persons nearest us, and geography will begin with that of the neighborhood of the school. Arithmetic will begin with the sums applicable to the pupils' homes. Having tried the method myself, I know that infinitely more knowledge can be given to the pupils through it, and without strain on them, than can be given through the orthodox method, within a given time.

"Knowledge of the alphabet should be treated as a separate subject altogether. The letters should be treated as pictures which the children will first be taught to recognize and name. Writing will follow as part of the drawing lesson. Instead of making daubs of their letters, pupils should be able to make perfect copies of the models placed before them. They would not, therefore, be called upon to draw the letters till they had acquired control over their fingers and the pen.

"It is criminal to stunt the mental growth of a child by letting him know only as much as he can get through a book which he can incoherently read in a year. We do not realize that if a child was cut off from the home life and was merely doomed to the school, he would be a perfect dunce for several years. He picks up information and language unconsciously through his home, not in the school-room. Hence do we experience the immense difference between pupils belonging to cultured homes and those belonging to uncouth homes, which are no homes in reality.

"In the scheme I have adumbrated, the schoolmaster is expected to treat his occupation seriously and feel one with his pupils. I know that, in putting the scheme into operation, the want of schoolmasters of the right type is the greatest difficulty. But we shall not get the right type till we have made the right beginning.

"I must postpone the consideration of the stage when we have to arm the pupils with books."

These principles enunciated by Gandhi are in conformity with the most advanced pedagogy of America—physical examination, story-telling, the conversational method, the visual method of instruction, education rooted in social experience and flowing back into social experience more enriched and vitalized.

It is poetic justice that the children of the underprivileged in India should be today the recipients of education based upon the most up-to-date pedagogical principles. The above statement on pedagogy alone is sufficient to entitle Gandhi to be considered the father of modern education in India. The world may profitably study Gandhi's pedagogy and watch the results of its application in contemporary India.[3]

Mahatma Gandhi's views on methods of teaching are, as we have noted, in conformity with the most advanced pedagogy of the Western world, but the end of education as visualized by him is in consonance with the ideals of "our ancient [Hindu] school system."[4] Considering Occidental civilization as "materialistic" and as a "nine days' wonder," Gandhi does not put much stock in the ideals of education propagated by the "victims" of that civilization. Taking his cue from Edward Carpenter, the Mahatma regards Western civilization as a "disease," whose chief symptom is irreligion.[5]

"Civilization," according to Mahatma Gandhi, "is that mode of conduct which points out to man the path of duty. Performance of duty and observance of morality are convertible terms. To observe morality is to attain mastery over our mind and our passions. So doing, we know ourselves. The Gujarati equivalent for civilization is 'good conduct.' "[6]

"Mastery over our mind and our passions"—yes, self-discipline, self-rule, *Swaraj*—that must be the end-product of true civilization, and the ideal of education. Instead of promoting self-discipline, modern civilization prompts its votaries to learn ever newer and more efficient ways of circumventing the restraints imposed by nature and society. Instead of holding up good health as the immediate as well as the ultimate ideal, modern civilization concentrates upon healing sickness by multiplying hospitals.

"A multiplicity of hospitals," says the Mahatma, "is no test of civilization. It is rather a symptom of decay even as a multiplicity of *Pinjrapoles* [hospitals for cattle] is a symptom of the indifference to the welfare of the cattle by the people in whose midst they are brought into being. Let us be concerned chiefly with the prevention of diseases rather than with their cure. The science of sanitation is infinitely more ennobling, though more difficult of execution, than the science of healing. I regard the present system of medicine as black magic, because it tempts people to put an undue importance on the body and practically ignores the spirit within. Investigate the laws concerning the health of the spirit and you will find that they will yield startling results even with reference to the cure of the body. The present science of medicine is divorced from religion. A man who attends to his daily *Namaz* or his *Gayatri* in the proper spirit need never fall ill. A clean spirit must build a clean body." (*Namaz and Gayatri are Mohammedan and Hindu forms of worship and prayer respectively; both require certain postures and intense concentration of mind.—H. T. M.*) [7]

Not only does modern civilization put a premium upon the multiplication of meliorative agencies such as hospitals but it also preaches the gospel of the good life in terms of a multiplicity of material goods. The more wants you have and the more goods you possess, the more civilized you are supposed to be. Such is the nature of Occidental civilization.

The business of the machinery of formal education the world over, from the standpoint of culture, is twofold: to propagate the values inherent in the particular culture, and to give lead in the creation of new values. The latter function of education is usually forgotten by the administrators of formal education. By the very logic of the situation, therefore, Western education cannot help teaching the cult of more wants, material prosperity, greed, bodily ease, circumvention (beating) of the laws if one can get by with it.

2. Gandhi's Definition of Primary and Higher Education

Referring specifically to "primary" and "higher" education, Mahatma Gandhi says: [8]

"What is the meaning of education? If it simply means a knowledge of letters, it is merely an instrument; and an instrument may be well used or abused. The same instrument that may be used to cure a patient may be used to take his life, and so may a knowledge of letters. [*That is to say, if a knowledge of letters were imparted without reference to the entelechy, to the implicit destiny, of man.*—H. T. M.] We daily observe that many men abuse it [i.e., their knowledge of letters] and very few make good use of it. . . .

"The ordinary meaning of education is a knowledge of letters. To teach boys reading, writing and arithmetic is called primary education. A peasant earns his bread honestly. He has ordinary knowledge of the world. He knows fairly well how he should behave toward his parents, his wife, his children and his fellow-villagers. He understands and observes the rules of morality. But he cannot write his name."

Is such a farmer, asks Gandhi in effect, to be considered uneducated? It is his contention that the illiterate peasant may be truly said to have had "primary" education because he duly fulfils his functions as a member of society.

"Now let us take higher education," continues Gandhi.[9] "I have learned Geography, Astronomy, Algebra, Geometry, etc. What of that? In what way have I benefited myself or those around me? Why have I learned these things? Professor Huxley has thus defined education: 'That man I think has had a liberal education who has been so trained in youth that his body is the ready servant of his will and does with ease and pleasure all the work that as a mechanism it is capable of; whose intellect is a clear, cold logic engine with all its parts of equal strength and in smooth working order; . . . whose mind is stored with a knowledge of the fundamental truths of nature; . . . whose passions are trained to come to heel by a vigorous will, the ready servant of a tender conscience; . . . who has learned to hate all vileness and to respect others as himself. Such an one and no other, I conceive, has had a liberal education, for he is in harmony with nature. He will make the best of her and she of him.'

"If this be true education, I must emphatically say that the sciences enumerated above I have never been able to use for controlling my senses. Therefore, whether you take elementary education or higher education, it is not required for the main thing. It does not make of us men. It does not enable us to do our duty." *

3. ENDS AND MEANS OF EDUCATION

What is "the main thing" that man must strive for, that civilization should uphold, that education should foster? The answer is: "Character-building," which used to have "the first place in our ancient school system." Yes, "character-building"—"that is primary education. A building erected on that foundation will last." 10

Character-building means "making of us men"; the "enabling us to do our duty"; "mastery over our mind and our passions." He who is master of himself is master of the universe. The Occident has made a fetish of freedom without fully understanding the meaning of freedom. Freedom does not consist in unlim-

---

* This was written in 1909 and, on the whole, Gandhi remained faithful to this point of view. While throughout his life he consistently underrated the value of formal education as it was being imparted in the India of his day, in later life Gandhi somewhat modified his harsh criticism of formal education. Thus, in 1921, dedicating a Medical College established to promote Hindu,. Muslim, and Western medical lore and practice, Gandhi went out of his way to "pay my humble tribute to the spirit of research that fires the modern scientist" (*Sermon on the Sea*, p. xxii). Again, in 1925, he said: "I value education in the different sciences. Our children cannot have too much of chemistry and physics" (*Young India*, March 12, 1925).

ited, aimless indulgence of one's whims and desires. If every motorist insisted on driving his car on the road wherever he pleased—i.e., on the right or the left or the center—there would be no "freedom" for any motorist to travel over the highways of this country with safety. Freedom, in other words, like every proper expression of human behavior, is in terms of a frame of reference, in terms of certain objectives and loyalties.

Freedom, according to Mahatma Gandhi, consists in *the capacity to impose restraints upon one's self.* The great German philosopher Nietzsche, likewise, defined freedom in similar terms. If freedom, thus defined, were held up as an objective before pupils, the problem of discipline would vanish instantaneously. But before this conception of freedom can be held up as a worthy objective by our educators, the dominant ideology of Occidental civilization shall have to be changed. Not a multiplication of wants but a renunciation of wants; not self-indulgence but self-denial; not beating the law but imposing restraints from within in conformity with the objective reality—not until these ideals become woven into the fabric of a civilization can its educational machinery preach them, and make them vital in the lives of pupils!

That physical, mental, and spiritual development should go hand in hand is a cardinal tenet of the Mahatma's philosophy of education. Let me quote a passage that bids fair to become classic: [11]

"I hold that true education of the intellect can only come through a proper exercise of the bodily organs, e.g., hands, feet, ears, nose, etc. In other words, an intelligent use of the bodily organs in a child provides the best and quickest way of developing his intellect. But unless the development of the mind and body goes hand-in-hand with a corresponding awakening of the soul, the former alone would prove to be a poor lopsided affair. By spiritual training I mean education of the heart. A proper and all-round development of the mind, therefore, can take place only when it proceeds *pari passu* with the education of the physical and spiritual faculties of the child. They constitute an indivisible whole. According to this theory, therefore, it would be a gross fallacy to suppose that they can be developed piecemeal or independently of one another."

Whenever he has had an opportunity to think on the subject or to write upon it or to express views on it, Gandhi has always approached education from the standpoint of character-building. He can never think of education except in terms of the formation of character. Interesting light is thrown upon this phase of Gandhi's pedagogy by the answers he gave to certain questions put to him by the eminent American educator Dr. Carleton Washburne, Superintendent of the Winnetka Public School System. The interview between Gandhi and Washburne took place in the midst of political turmoil, in the Winter of 1931, when Gandhi was engaged in the trying negotiations for a Pact of Truce with Lord Irwin (now Halifax), who was then Governor-General of India. Let me reproduce the interview in the form of questions and answers.

Q. "What is your goal in education when India obtains self-rule?"

A. "Character-building. . . . I would try to develop courage, strength, virtue, the ability to forget oneself in working toward great aims.

"This is more important than literacy; academic learning is only a means to this greater end. That is why India's great lack of literacy, deplorable as it is, does not appal me nor make me feel that India is unfit for self-rule."

Q. "Would you try to bring about any specific kind of social organization through education?"

A. "I should feel that if we succeed in building the character of the individual, society will take care of itself. I would be quite willing to trust the organization of society to individuals so developed."

Q. "In developing the new national spirit in India would you like to make patriotic feelings so strong that duty to one's country would be a higher good than obeying one's personal conscience?"

A. "I hope that will never be. One's own inner convictions come first always. But in a nation where character is developed among all individuals, there can be no conflict between the dictates of one's own conscience and those of the State."

Q. "In the attempt to build character would you present biographical and historical material in such a way as to inculcate ideals and attitudes, or would you hold to objective reality and historical accuracy?"

A. "You mean, Would I follow the English or American example? [Chuckling] I hope not. The truth must come first always." *

Q. "In developing the national spirit in India today would you subordinate internationalism?"

A. "I hope we will never use our nationalism to exploit other nations, but that our nationalism is only a prelude to internationalism."

Thus ended the all-too-brief interview, as recorded by Dr. Washburne.[12]

Gandhi's philosophy of education may be summarized in a sentence: if we can develop each child's spirit and ability, we have done all that education can do. But this statement needs to be qualified. The child cannot develop his spirit and ability *in vacuo*. He must engage in all sorts of activities and manipulations and participate in the social process in order to develop his spirit and ability. You cannot, for instance, develop the ability to read without reading *something*. The content of this *something* that you give the child to read must be in consonance with the spirit premised by the educator—by Gandhi, in this case. Let the accessory material, reading matter, inculcate values—for example, *Ahimsa* and Truth!

The philosophy of non-violent resistance, grounded upon

---

* Gandhi here confuses polemical writings of popular authors with objective writings of historians. To be sure, cultural bias is inevitable even in the most objective historical writing; but, on the whole, English and American historians are as objective as any others in the world, indeed a shade *more* objective than others, including Hindese historians. Had he been as familiar with the writings of other Western nations as he had been with those of Britain and America, Gandhi would have castigated in no uncertain terms the distortion of truth practiced by ideological totalitarian States, whose historians must "write history" to order.—H. T. M.

Truth and *Ahimsa*, says Gandhi, "is the noblest and best education. It should come, not after the ordinary literary education of
children; it should precede it. It will not be denied that a child,
before it begins to write its alphabet and to gain worldly knowledge, should know what the soul is, what truth is, what love is,
what powers are latent in the soul. It should be an essential of
real education that a child should learn that, in the struggle of
life, it can easily conquer hate by love, untruth by truth, violence
by self-suffering. It was because I felt the force of this truth that
I endeavored to train the children at Tolstoy Farm, and then at
Phoenix [both in South Africa], along these lines. . . ." [13]

At the Satyagraha Ashram (Abode of Truth-Living), at
Sabarmati, near Ahmedabad, founded in 1916, all the members,
young as well as old, were required, as pointed out in Chapter
Three, to take the eightfold vow: (1) truth, (2) *Ahimsa*, (3)
celibacy, (4) control of the palate, (5 non-thieving, i.e., non-possession of superfluous worldly goods, (6) non-possession of riches,
(7) *Swadeshi* (i.e., use of homespun garments and homemade
goods), (8) fearlessness. The Ashram was conceived as a sort of
boarding school both for adults and children. It ran a small model
dairy and tannery and carried on truck gardening on a small scale.
The dignity of labor was emphasized and inculcated. Politics, economics, and sociology were taught "in a religious spirit." In 1920
the function of formal education was transferred from the Ashram
to the Gujarat Vidyapith—i.e., to the Gujarat National University
—about a mile away.

As for the religious spirit in education, religion, as conceived
by Gandhi, is not what "you will get after reading all the Scriptures of the world. Religion is not really what is grasped by the
brain, but a heart grasp." [14]

Such is the pattern of the "school"—of "the boarding
school," of the "Ashram"—that Gandhi conducted for a decade
and a half in India. Its emphasis on the training of the heart and
the emotions is obvious. The Satyagraha Ashram (converted into
a Harijan Training School since 1930–1931) may indeed be said
to have been a translation of the forest-universities of ancient
India to the industrial-urban India of our age.

True to the genius of India, Gandhi established his Ashram not in a big city but away from it—on the periphery of Ahmedabad, the Manchester of India. Such a location enabled "students" to enjoy all the advantages of forest-universities of ancient India. Education here meant, in the first place, a living of life in terms of the social processes incident to the corporate and cooperative living of the members of the Ashram. In the second place, away from the passing phantoms of speed-mad urban centers, the "students" were in the world but not of the world. In the third place, untrammelled by the bondage of wants, desires, and superfluous appetites, the students could study objectively the various aspects of this *Samsara,* the on-going phenomenon we call the universe, under competent instructors—all this to the end that at the end of their discipleship, of their apprenticeship, they may be enabled the better to participate in the continuum of the cultural process and dedicate themselves to the uplift of humanity.

Since he actively espoused the cause of the Harijans in 1932 and threw all his energies into the crusade for the abolition of untouchability, Gandhi was pressed by force of circumstances to do a great deal of thinking on the concrete problems of education —education of the adult, education of the young ones, education of the children of the privileged classes, education of underprivileged children. Through this period of intense searching of the heart, through this period of inward storm and stress in the midst of the political quiescence of the thirties, the Mahatma was led on to enunciate definitively his philosophy of education containing not a few revolutionary ideas:

(1) That education shall be conceived as a continuous, growing process; (2) that the attempt be made to impart a comprehensive world-view to every child during the first seven years of schooling; (3) that all learning shall take place around a dominant interest, such as a basic craft; (4) that education shall be self-supporting through the products of the child's craftsmanship.

The Mahatma was not given to rhetorical flourishes. He wrote and uttered unadorned words. But behind those simple words it is not difficult to discern the spirit of one who is consumed by a burning desire to serve childhood, underprivileged childhood in particular.

To make each child self-reliant, fearless, competent to weather the storms of life, upright, honorable, self-respecting, and respected by others, fit to take his place as a worthy member of the nation, capable of bearing witness to *Ahimsa* and Truth, to peace on earth and goodwill among men—such is the goal of Gandhi's pedagogy.

"Suffer little children to come unto Me," said the Master of Galilee; "of such is the Kingdom of Heaven!"

4. THE WARDHA SCHEME OF EDUCATION

In the field of education, Gandhi's name will always remain associated with the Wardha Scheme of Education.[15] How to make education, especially in a poor country like India, *self-supporting* presented a challenge to Gandhi. He came forth with a bold, revolutionary answer. Gandhi's two main propositions may be stated in his own words: [16]

"(1) Primary education, extending over a period of seven years or longer, and covering all the subjects up to the matriculation standard, except English, plus a vocation used as a vehicle for drawing out the minds of boys and girls in all departments of knowledge, should take the place of what passes today under the name of Primary, Middle and High School education.

"(2) Such education, taken as a whole, can and must be self-supporting; in fact, self-support is the acid test of its reality."

Gandhi proposes that *the trade or craft or skilled occupation, chosen by the pupil, shall serve as the dominant motive around which all learning shall be integrated* to the end that mind, body, and heart may be cultivated in a balanced manner, culminating in the formation of a noble character. The tools of learning, contends the Mahatma, may not be imparted without due regard for their ethical connotations. A tool may be either used or abused. Learning should have as its aim nothing short of noble character.

For two days in October, 1937, on the twenty-second and the twenty-third, a conference of leading educators and Ministers

of Education was held at Wardha under the chairmanship of
Mahatma Gandhi. Four propositions were submitted by Gandhi
to the Conference:

(1) The present system of education with its emphasis upon
English is ill-suited to India and should be revised. (2) A seven-
year schooling program imparting "general knowledge," less English, plus a vocation, should be substituted in its place. (3) "For
the all-round development of boys and girls all training should so
far as possible be given through a profit-yielding vocation," the
State to guarantee "employment in the vocations learnt" and to
"buy their [pupils'] manufactures at prices fixed by the State"
itself. (4) "Higher education" in arts and sciences "should be left
to private enterprise."

The Conference accepted the Mahatma's propositions *in toto*
as a frame of reference. A committee was appointed under the
chairmanship of Dr. Zakir Husain, German-trained, to make a
report on the ways and means to embody these suggestions into a
working program.

On December 11, 1937, the Zakir Husain Committee
made its report. It reiterated the fundamental postulates of
Gandhi's pedagogy and set forth certain "basic principles" and
"objectives" for the reconstruction of the curriculum. We may call
this report the Wardha Scheme of Education. Accepting the
tenets of modern pedagogy which "commends the idea of educating children through some suitable form of productive work," the
Zakir Husain Committee recommends the adoption of any or all
of the following industries as basic craft: spinning and weaving,
carpentry, agriculture, fruit and vegetable gardening, leather
work, and "any other craft for which local and geographical conditions are favorable and which satisfies the conditions [of modern pedagogy]."

The purpose of the basic craft as an integral part of the curriculum is "not primarily the production of craftsmen able to
practise some craft *mechanically,* but rather the exploitation, for
educative purposes, of the resources implicit in craft work." The
pursuit of the basic craft is intended to "inspire the *method* of

teaching all other subjects," inasmuch as "the craft or productive work . . . [is] rich in educative possibilities, . . . [having] natural points of correlation with important human activities and interests, and extending into the whole content of the school curriculum." Furthermore, the practice of the basic craft should emphasize "cooperative activity, planning, accuracy, initiative and individual responsibility in learning."

In the Wardha Scheme of Education, say the authors of the report, there is implicit the ideal of citizenship. "The scheme envisages the idea of a cooperative community, in which the motive of social service will dominate all the activities of children during the plastic years of childhood and youth." All education during the seven-year period of study shall be imparted, according to the new scheme, through the medium of the mother tongue of the province, while Hindese (Hindusthani), which the All-India National Congress, under Gandhi's leadership, had been striving to make into the *lingua franca* of India, shall be among the required subjects for graduation.

Let us now address ourselves to a brief investigation of whether or not the central thesis of the Wardha Scheme of Education is valid. Broadly speaking, four fundamental pedagogic tenets are formulated: (1) The artificial distinctions between primary, middle, and high school shall be abolished, and education shall be conceived as a continuous, growing process without compartmental divisions. (2) The period of education shall be seven years —from the seventh year to the fourteenth—alike for boys and girls. (3) All learning shall be integrated around a basic craft or a basic set of crafts, depending upon the aptitudes of children and the needs of our society. (4) The child as an apprentice shall, during the seven years of study, render enough goods and services to offset the major portion of his cost of education, if indeed not the whole of it.

Let us take these items one by one:

1. The academic setup the world over suffers too much from artificial divisions and compartmental arrangements—the 8:4:4 ratio in the United States and the 5:3:4:4 ratio in India for

elementary, secondary, and higher education. A child with the intellectual attainments of a high school scholar is condemned to remain in the elementary division if he has not served out the full term of eight years. This is an injustice to society and a punishment to the precocious child. Under the circumstances, whatever frees us from the slavery of the time ratio is a desirable step in pedagogy. Our problem today the world over is to free men's minds from the tyranny of neat schemes based upon the time element involved in schooling. If the Wardha Scheme accomplishes only this questioning of the traditional ratio idea of education, it has merit enough.

2. By concentrating upon the first years of education as though that were the whole field of education, certain advantages are to be gained. The present-day compartmentalized system of education is organized on the theory that when the pupil has gone through the 8:4:4 period of study, he will have a nodding acquaintance with the universe. For instance, certain subjects are never brought to the attention of the child in the elementary school on the plea that they are beyond the comprehension of the young learner. These "tabooed" or "reserved" subjects are to be pursued at higher levels only. Let me put it in a slightly different form: Elementary schooling is conceived as a preparation for secondary schooling which itself is conceived as a preparation for college training!

As a matter of fact, the majority of students do not go to high school (except in countries where high school education is also free and the age limit for school attendance is as high as sixteen or eighteen). Of those who attend high school the majority do not go to college. The very assumptions of the present system are thus defeated. The present system, evolved blindly, promises that a more or less comprehensive *Weltanschauung* will be experienced by the pupil only on condition that he shall go through the whole of the academic mill, including college training. What happens to the students who quit school after finishing the primary or elementary grades? Are they in a position to function as intelligent citizens? Decidedly not.

Inasmuch as the majority of pupils, under present conditions, are not expected to go to college, the Wardha Scheme, by concentrating its attention upon the first years of school, is calculated to turn out better men and women than does the present academic setup whose logical terminus is graduation from college.

3. The outstanding pedagogical discovery of the twentieth century (rather, rediscovery, for the principle had been formulated previously by keen educators in the past) is that learning shall be "carried over" from one field into another and integrated around a dominant interest. Different patches of information and bits of knowledge, before they can become significant parts of learning, must be related to a dominant frame of reference. What I learn, for instance, in biology and chemistry I should be able to refer to physics and sociology. The new interest in the study of human ecology is a fitting illustration of what I have in mind.

Let us say the basic craft is hand spinning. What cannot an intelligent teacher do to stimulate the child's inquisitiveness, to lay bare before him the working of the cosmic process, with the aid of the humble spinning wheel? Spinning wheel: yarn, weaving, cloth, types of dress, morals and manners and clothing, home furnishings, drapes, household management. Spinning wheel as machine: motive power, organization of factories, labor, capital, production, distribution, consumption, the standard of living. Spinning wheel and income: food, clothing, shelter, urban society versus rural life. Spinning wheel, the wood it is made of: the tree, plant life, the principles of botany, the principles of biology, zoology, etc. Spinning wheel and friction involved in spinning: rust on the needle, metal and wood compared and contrasted, physics and chemistry; the wheel, the basic factor in transportation and in large-scale machinery: the history of transportation. The wheel a circle: geometry. The wheel's rhythm: the rhythm of the seasons, the cosmic cycles.

The mysteries of the universe can be explored, under competent guidance, with the spinning wheel as a starting point. And not the spinning wheel alone—you may take any other tool for any other basic craft and formulate steps leading to the study of mathematics, astronomy, physics, chemistry, biology, psychology, sociology (including all the social sciences, as well as all the arts, all the philosophies, all the religious systems). The only catch is: Are there competent teachers who themselves have experienced an integrated *Weltanschauung*? I am afraid India's first job shall have to be to educate not the child, but the adult—the teachers and the parents—the fundamental problem the world over!

Leaving aside the technical problem of teacher-training, one modification—and an important one—might be made in the formulation of the third part of the Wardha Scheme of Education. I would not say, "All learning shall be integrated around a basic *craft*"; rather would I say, "All learning shall be organized, co-ordinated, and integrated around a dominant *interest*." The dominant interest in India as elsewhere is just twofold: the promotion of livelihood, including the standard of living in the comprehensive sense of the term, and the inculcation of civic responsibility. This way of formulating the problem would remove the taint of crass materialism from the Wardha Scheme without lessening the emphasis upon the learning of a craft, trade, or skill as an instrumentality for the promotion of livelihood.

4. Impoverished India may yet make a revolutionary contribution to educational theory and practice. Let us remember that Pestalozzi's grand principles of pedagogy were evolved while he was striving to serve the *underprivileged* of Switzerland, and that Montessori's pedagogy was evolved from her efforts at serving the underprivileged of Italy. In his endeavors to serve the underprivileged of India Mahatma Gandhi was led to enunciate the most revolutionary part of his pedagogy. Yes, self-support must be the acid test of the reality of our education.

The adult has to do socially useful work. Why should we, then, discourage the child from doing socially useful work in his formative years? The principle is thoroughly sound. I must, however, confess that the curriculum drawn up by the Zakir Husain Committee is capable of a great deal of adjustment here and there.

A school day of five hours and thirty minutes, suggests the Committee, may be divided into the following periods of study:

Subject	Hours	Minutes
1. The basic craft	3	20
2. Music, drawing, arithmetic	—	40
3. Mother tongue	—	40
4. Social studies and general science	—	30
5. Physical training	—	10
6. Recess	—	10

The Wardha Scheme is sure to be criticized by our educators from the varying standpoints of idealism, realism, and pragmatism. Pedagogues are apt to quarrel, for a long time to come, whether this curriculum is valid or invalid, whether it is lopsided or balanced. I would say it is substantially sound, even though it needs a great real of revamping. The program cannot be endorsed unqualifiedly, and the curriculum would be deemed entirely invalid if the principle of integration of learning around the basic craft were not honored in the classroom.

Furthermore, athletics, dancing, recreation—activities that promote the joy of living—must be emphasized much more in India than elsewhere as an offset against the Hindese people's tendency to withdrawal and seriousness. Nor may the study of English be entirely eliminated during the seven-year period of schooling. Two years of English, taught scientifically, would make the Hindese scholar a better master of that language than the present regimen of eleven years of English teaching has succeeded in doing.

A note of warning is in order. We are not going to solve the problem of education by putting the child into school at the age of seven as envisaged by Gandhi. The child's patterns of thinking and behavior have already been formed by that time by home influences. The fundamental problem in India or elsewhere is to regenerate the home and to bring the home, the school, and the community into harmonious relationships with one another.

CHAPTER SEVEN

THE APOSTLE OF NON-VIOLENCE

1. Contemporary Appraisals of Gandhi

IN HIS greetings to Mahatma Gandhi on his seventy-fifth birthday, Albert Einstein called him "a leader of his people, unsupported by any outward authority; a politician whose success rests not upon craft nor mastery of technical devices, but simply on the convincing power of his personality; a victorious fighter who has always scorned the use of force; a man of wisdom and humility, armed with resolve and inflexible consistency, who has devoted all his strength to the uplifting of his people and the betterment of their lot; a man who has confronted the brutality of Europe with the dignity of the simple human being, and thus at all times risen superior." "Generations to come," continues Einstein, "will scarce believe that such a one as this ever in flesh and blood walked upon this earth." [1]

And here is a noteworthy statement by Mr. J. Z. Hodgend in *The Glasgow Herald* in the early twenties, when India was in the grip of the non-violent non-cooperation movement: [2]

"He [Gandhi] is the soul of India in revolt, the spirit of Indian discontent, the assertion of the East's equality with the West, the most powerful and at the same time the most puzzling personality in India today. . . . He baffles classification. Here, for example, are a few estimates that came within my own knowledge. 'Sir, he is a God,' was the reverent verdict of a Bengali stationmaster; 'God has given only one Gandhi Sahib in this millennium,' was the fine tribute of an unlettered villager; 'Gandhi is our Mahatma' (our superman), was the faith of a student disciple; 'This man reminds me of the Apostle Paul,' said a shrewd Government official who had evidently been to Sunday School in his youth. 'Beware of Gandhi,' wrote a valued friend. 'He is a revolutionary of a most dangerous type.' I have heard him further described as a 'charlatan,' a 'madman,' a 'visionary,' a 'menace to British rule'; an 'astute politician who hides his real designs under a mask of guileless simplicity'; an 'irresponsible and unscrupulous agitator,' a 'country cousin,' the 'savior of his country,' and the 'egregious Mr. Gandhi' (who is a 'thrawn devil'). This, then, is no common man, be he revolutionary or evolutionary, prophet or politician, saint or sinner, agitator or statesman, madman or wiseman, savior or wrecker, mere man or superman; come he in peace or come he in war, he arrests attention and demands a hearing."

Forgetting for the moment the flowery language of poetry, Tagore at about the same time paid this tribute in simple prose: "Gandhi is a saint and saints have still a chance in India." [3]

Perhaps the most penetrating analysis of Gandhi's mode of operation was made by Gilbert Murray (*The Hibbert Journal* 1917–1918): [4] "Persons in power should be very careful how they deal with a man who cares nothing for sensual pleasure, nothing for riches, nothing for comfort or praise or promotion, but is simply determined to do what he believes to be right. He is a dangerous and uncomfortable enemy because his body, which you can always conquer, gives so little purchase upon his soul."

2. GANDHI'S CONTRIBUTIONS TO INDIA

Gandhi was not born with a sense of mission in life; it grew upon him gradually and imperceptibly during his South African sojourn of two decades. As we have seen, he developed an experimental turn of mind very early in life; but in his boyhood days he was, as he told me, a "darkop," i.e., a coward. He used to be afraid of the dark; this fear shamed him poignantly, especially when he discovered that his wife of the same age, fourteen years old, would venture forth fearlessly in the dark. It is a far cry from the coward of fourteen to the brave, fearless hero of forty, leader of his oppressed compatriots in South Africa. Is there a formula for converting a coward into a hero? Gandhi's life gives a telling answer to the question: forgetting one's petty interests, losing one's self in the service of others, giving loyalty unto death to values and principles cherished as eternal verities. Psychiatrists are today telling us that a great many personality disorders may be overcome by forgetting the narrow interests of the self, by developing an outreaching personality mindful of the interests of others, by cultivating love for our fellowmen, by giving allegiance to a cause transcending one's petty self. In other words, he who is willing to lose his life in the service of others is rewarded with life abundant on this planet—and in the other world, if one believes in the other world.

As a specialist in *Ahimsa* and Truth, Gandhi has made the world his debtor by his actual demonstration of the moral equivalent of war. Specifically, so far as India was concerned, he made a fear-ridden people fearless. The prison-houses and the gallows which used to awe the people were transformed into holy shrines. He endowed non-violence with power. He taught the virtue of self-discipline and self-purification to the individual, and disciplined, organized action to the masses for overcoming social, economic, and political ills. He brought religion—not creedal religion but essential religion—into politics and set about the task of spiritualizing politics with measurable success. Not only did he uplift a degraded people into a self-respecting nation but he ennobled the tone of public life. Handling of public funds, he would say, was a trust which could not be betrayed. He himself would spend hours, if need be, accounting for the last penny and would hold his followers responsible with the same stern discipline. While the Hindese are not necessarily better than other peoples, Gandhi's example and discipline for the most part weaned them away from graft and corruption. And he imparted to his followers a concern for the well-being of the underprivileged. Today communism has a feeble foothold in India, because the present government of India under Gandhi's followers, Nehru and others, is genuinely concerned with the well-being of the oppressed masses. Wherever such concern is lacking, the inroads of communism present a deadly threat.

3. ASOKA, PENN, AND GANDHI

There have been three significant attempts in human history "to spiritualize politics." The Buddhist Emperor Asoka of India (reigned 273 B.C.–232 B.C.), after successfully overcoming warring princes, banished warfare from his far-flung domains in an attempt to practise *Ahimsa* in statecraft. The experiment was successful during his long reign, but upon his death the Empire disintegrated and fell victim to barbarians from within and from without.

William Penn, founder of Pennsylvania, and the early Quakers or Friends likewise tried the experiment in "holy obedience," and practised *Ahimsa* in statecraft. In the sordid relations between the "white" colonists and the "red" Indians, the Quakers of Pennsylvania present a striking illustration of honorable and fair dealings on both sides. So long as the majority in the legislature was composed of Quakers and Mennonites, politics were guided by religious concerns. But when the legislature of Pennsylvania began to have a non-Quaker majority, the Quakers found themselves in an embarrassing position. They believed in majority rule, but the majority did not believe in *Ahimsa*. The Quakers felt they would incur a share of responsibility for military appropriations, regardless of whether they refrained from voting or opposed the measures. So they retreated from politics, at least so far as representation by election in government was concerned. Two exceptions may be noted. Herbert Hoover, the only Quaker who ever chose to run for the highest office in this country, was elected President of the United States on his record as Relief Administrator in Belgium. Hoover the Quaker believed in the Friends' testimony of *Ahimsa,* but Hoover the President had to be the Commander-in-Chief of the armed forces of the U. S. A. Still more recently, Professor Paul H. Douglas of the University of Chicago, a Quaker by persuasion, ran for the office of United States Senator from Illinois and was elected. But then, while he believed in the validity of *Ahimsa* as a way of life, Mr. Douglas the Quaker had already participated in World War II as a Marine.

The supreme dilemma facing the Quakers is the problem of conscience versus the State machinery as it has been operating. The Religious Society of Friends as a body has resolved the dilemma, thus far, by not seeking representation in government but by undertaking activities calculated to transform the nature of the State. Wars and rumors of war, they hope, would be banished from relations among nations; then they would be happy to seek election to the legislatures.

Retreating from statecraft as they did, the Quakers have been ever willing to use legal and political means to redress wrong whenever possible; to educate the public and create public opinion favorable to their "concern"; to seek rectification of wrong by legislation if possible; to engage in social work and philanthropic activity with a view to feeding the enhungered, clothing the naked, sheltering the homeless; to work for healing and reconciliation in areas of tension; to embark upon the ministry of goodwill and love, and to bear witness to their reliance upon the Inner Light and to their opposition to war and violence.

This phase of the Friends' activity would be called by Mahatma Gandhi "the constructive program."

Gandhi's own task was simpler than that of the Quakers in a free society. He had no responsibility for the running of the State machinery; he did not, could not, participate in the making of national policy. Possibilities of compromise with *Ahimsa* were, therefore, much more limited, and could be completely eliminated by the simple device of wholehearted allegiance to *Ahimsa*. And that is precisely what Gandhi did. Himself an exemplar of *Ahimsa*, he called upon his people to give non-violent battle to the British Raj. But Gandhi was never chicken-hearted. His inner integrity would not permit him to dodge the issue of the demands of *Ahimsa* versus the demands of the State. Thus in his reply to an open letter from Rev. B. de Ligt, he said: [5] "There is no defense for my conduct [*participation in the British-Boer War, the Zulu Rebellion, World War I*] weighed only in the scales of *Ahimsa*. . . . But even after introspection during all these years, I feel that in the circumstances in which I found myself I was bound to adopt the course I did during the Boer War and the Great European War and, for that matter, the so-called Zulu 'Rebellion' of Natal in 1906."

Since life is governed by a multitude of forces, one must choose between possible alternative courses of behavior. This choice must contribute to the furtherance of the ultimate value or values one holds dear. But Gandhi claimed for his conduct that "it was, in the instances cited, actuated in the interests of non-violence." As a "confirmed war resister," he had refused to give himself training in the use of arms. "But as long as I lived under a system of government based on force and voluntarily partook of the many facilities and privileges it created for me, I was bound to help that government to the extent of my ability when it was engaged in a war, unless I non-cooperated with that government and renounced to the utmost of my capacity the privileges it offered me." If Gandhi felt such a deep sense of obligation to an alien government, how much more compelling is the obligation owed by the citizen to the State in a democracy in time of crisis? Here is a challenge to American pacifists. Chivalry is an indispensable ingredient of *Satyagraha*. The American pacifist need not take up arms to kill others, if his conscience so dictates; but he should refrain from embarrassing his government, in times of crisis, by unchivalrous acts.

The problem was still deeper than that for Gandhi. He who believed in the sacredness of *all* life would not and did not hesitate "to instigate and direct an attack on the monkeys in order to save the crops." Since he could not abstract himself from society and since agriculture was an essential human pursuit, "in fear and trembling, in humility and penance, I therefore participate in the injury inflicted on the monkeys, hoping some day to find a way out." It was with some such consideration that he had participated in "the three acts of war." "[Today, however] I should not voluntarily participate in its [government's] wars, and I should risk imprisonment and even the gallows if I were forced to take up arms or otherwise take part in its military operations."

Even this affirmation did "not solve the riddle." What would be his position under a Hindese national government? "If there

were a national government, whilst I should not take any direct
part in any war, I can conceive occasions when it would be my
duty to vote for the military training of those who wish to take
it. For I know that all its members do not believe in non-violence
to the extent I do. It is not possible to make a person or a society
non-violent by compulsion."

This statement was made in 1928. In 1931, outlining his
vision of a free India, he said, "We should have the smallest army
imaginable." And when India sent troops into Kashmir to repel
the aggression of tribesmen and Pakistan "volunteer" troops,
Gandhi said the Government of India had done so with his con-
currence if not with his blessing.

This raises three questions: (1) Was Gandhi inconsistent?
(2) What was Gandhi's conception of the State? (3) Was Gandhi
a pacifist in the American sense of the term?

4. WAS GANDHI INCONSISTENT?

While he was an absolutist in his philosophy of life and in
his fundamental loyalties, Gandhi was a relativist and pragmatist
in his mode of operation. No situation was ever completely black
or white to him. He would view every event and episode from
several perspectives. For instance, war may be viewed from the
standpoint of slaughter of human beings, unarmed civilians as
well as armed soldiers; or from the standpoint of destruction of
property; or, yet, from the standpoint of loyalty to one's nation
and to one's cherished ideals; or from the standpoint of self-reali-
zation through self-sacrifice. Some engage in war from fear and
hate of the out-group; others from love of one's in-group. To some
war is an escape from the humdrum routine of daily life, to
others it is a crusade for righteousness.

Could a believer in *Ahimsa,* for instance, advocate participation in war and still remain consistent? Gandhi's answer was:
"My conception of *Ahimsa* impels me to dissociate myself from
almost every one of the activities I am engaged in. My soul refuses
to be satisfied so long as it is a helpless witness of a single wrong

or a single misery. But it is not possible for me, a weak, frail, miserable being, to mend every wrong or to hold myself free of blame for all the wrong I see. The spirit in me pulls one way, the flesh in me pulls in the opposite direction. . . . This struggle resolves itself into an incessant crucifixion of the flesh so that the spirit may become entirely free."

As for his recruiting campaign, Gandhi said that while he himself believed in *Ahimsa* the others did not, and were refusing to do their duty of assisting the government out of anger and malice, out of ignorance and weakness. "As a fellow worker, it became my duty to guide them aright. I, therefore, placed before them their clear duty, explained the doctrine of *Ahimsa* to them and let them make their choice which they did. I do not repent of my action in terms of *Ahimsa*. For, under *Swaraj*, too, I would not hesitate to advise those who would bear arms to do so and fight for the country." [6]

During one of my daily early morning walks with him in London, I too asked Gandhi concerning his inconsistencies and "Machiavellianism." "Bapuji, let us suppose you have an unsympathetic biographer. He could point to at least six or seven events in your life and so interpret them as to make you out to be not only inconsistent but also Machiavellian." Then I recounted, with special interpretation, six or seven such situations in Gandhi's life. He listened to me attentively and then, with a broad grin, said, "You forgot the latest two of my 'Machiavellian' acts!" And he pointed to two recent incidents susceptible of such interpretation. Then he said: "Of course, your unsympathetic biographer would be justified in misinterpreting me, as you suggest, that is, if he chose to do so. The facts do lend themselves to such representation or misrepresentation. But I would ask your unsympathetic biographer to go behind the facts and discover the motives in each case. In the situations we have been discussing, my motives were pure—there can be no disagreement on that; there may be debate on whether my judgments were sound. I should say that an act should be judged by the motive which inspired it. From an error in judgment redemption is possible; from an error in motivation redemption is difficult, if not well-nigh impossible."

5. Gandhi's Conception of the State

"For the sake of conscience, sacrifice all," said the *Mahabharata*. Gandhi approved the principle and lived it in his life. Like the early Christians, if he were confronted with a choice between loyalty to God or conscience and loyalty to the State, he would choose loyalty to God and conscience. Such an extreme situation never presented itself to Gandhi. Ordinarily, the authority of the State is to be accepted as a fact, and man's freedoms and responsibilities, rights and duties, must be worked out within the framework of the State. Just as the State has the obligation to make possible the good life for the citizen, on his part the citizen has the obligation to help in the maintenance and operation of the State in smooth order. The State must allow the utmost latitude and freedom to the individual; this it can do, said Gandhi, by the minimum amount of interference in the affairs of citizens.

Gandhi's attitudes toward the State are mixed: on the one hand, he wants a Welfare State with all the controls implicit in such a political order, and, on the other hand, he wants a *laissez faire* State. Proposing a toast to the British Empire in 1915, Gandhi said: [7] "I have been often asked how I, a determined opponent of modern civilization and an avowed patriot, could reconcile myself to loyalty to the British Empire of which India was such a large part; . . . I discovered that the British Empire had certain ideals with which I have fallen in love, and one of those ideals is that every subject of the British Empire has the freest scope possible for his energies and honor and whatever he thinks is due to his conscience. . . . I am no lover of any government, and I have more than once said that that government is best which governs least. And I have found that it is possible for me to be governed least under the British Empire. Hence my loyalty to the British Empire."

In 1922 this "farmer and weaver who was once a lawyer" pointed out at his trial that "to preach disaffection toward the existing system of government has become almost a passion with me." And at St. James's Palace in London, at the opening session of the Second Round Table Conference (1931), the Mahatma announced, "I would far rather be called a rebel than a subject." Gandhi's rebellion against the British Raj, in other words, was not a revolt against government or government authority as such; nor was the revolt motivated by the fact that the government was British and foreign. The compelling reason was Gandhi's conviction that the "existing government" was incapable of affording the Hindese citizen "the freest scope possible for his energies and honor and whatever he thinks is due to his conscience."

In spite of his proclaimed belief in the least government as being the best, Gandhi had nothing in common with anarchism. He, a rigid self-disciplinarian, had no hesitation in imposing the sternest discipline upon those who wanted to live and work with him. The Congress, which he dominated since 1920 until his martyrdom in 1948, functioned like a State within the State, with all the authority, discipline, and coercive powers of the government. He transformed the Congress from a talking body into an efficient businesslike organization. From time to time he would issue directives as to the conduct of the Satyagrahists. Gandhi was forever organizing, forever distributing authority, forever allocating power. Significantly, the terminology evolved by the Congress at the height of the civil disobedience movement (1930–1934) smacked of centralized authority and dictatorship: there were Congress "dictators" in actual power and as alternates at the national level and at the Provincial levels, all ready to carry forward the organized movement until arrested by the British authorities. An American correspondent referred to Gandhi as "the Paramount Power" in India.

Time and again Gandhi would criticize the government for not doing this or that thing which might contribute to the well-being of the masses. On the whole, however, I incline to the view that Gandhi's political philosophy was very much like that of our American pioneers: self-help and civic enterprise, rather than government intrusion. But in the heat of the battle, overcome by the despair and degradation of the masses, he tended to emphasize the role of the government in removing miseries.

Gandhi believed in democracy. His democracy would be not

a genuine democracy as we understand it but more like Plato's Republic, wherein the elite would administer the government by virtue of their desire and competence to serve the masses. He would not, for instance, even permit himself the luxury "to judge or scrutinize Ministerial decisions with the solemnity of a tribunal"; what right then would lesser citizens have to judge the actions of their chosen representatives? "I would be deeply distressed," said Gandhi, "if on every conceivable occasion every one of us were to be a law unto oneself and to scrutinize in golden scales every action of our future National Assembly. I would surrender my judgment in most matters to national representatives, taking particular care in making my choice of such representatives. I know that in no other manner would a democratic government be possible for one single day." [8]

6. WAS GANDHI A PACIFIST?

The problem of pacifism, i.e., complete renunciation of violent methods in the settlement of disputes, needs to be viewed at three levels: individual, group, and State.

In his famous editorial on "The Doctrine of the Sword" (*Young India,* August 11, 1920), Gandhi categorically affirmed that when there was "only a choice between cowardice and violence," he "would advise violence." [9] He would also say that when there was a choice between appeasement, a species of cowardice, and violence, he would advise violence. In regard to the behavior of an individual not wholeheartedly committed to non-violence, the use of violence in interpersonal relations for the vindication of right, or for the fending off of assault on an innocent person or on one's self, was not only permissible but would also become a duty. His son, for example, said Gandhi, could have used violence in warding off an attack on his father in 1908, if he was minded to use physical force.

According to Gandhi, there are three types of human beings, three possible types of response to an evil situation. First, there is the coward who, in order to save his skin, either flees from the danger or submits to injustice and evil. This is the despicable type. His departure from life would be no loss to mankind. Second, there is the heroic man who, in order to uphold his honor or to vindicate his position, is willing to take up the sword, and bravely kills or dies. This heroic type is to be preferred to the first type at all times. He brings glory to the human race. Third, there is the superior man who, in the full consciousness of his strength, is willing to forgive the evildoer, to redeem him, to convert him into a co-worker in the mending or the ending of the evil system. The Mahatma himself belonged to this third type, the superior type. Blessed are the peace-makers!

As to relations between group and group or between the group and an individual, resort to violence by the group should be condemned. Intergroup conflict on the plane of violence leads to social instability and to the weakening of the State. Group violence against an individual results in lynch law—a denial of the democratic process. Hence Gandhi believed in the efficient functioning of the State machinery as an agency for social change, for the harmonizing of conflicting intergroup interests, for the adjudication of conflicts between individual and individual, between the individual and the group.

How about the behavior of the State itself, which is at once the most important institution in society and the largest in-group within a nation? The State, from one standpoint, is the association of all the citizens for the due exercise of power and authority, regulation and control, adjudication and administration, rights and responsibilities, duties and obligations, devolving upon each citizen as a member of society. Historically, the State has been performing three specific functions: (1) serving as a mechanism for the distribution of goods and services, (2) serving as a mechanism for the resolution of conflict among its "members," (3) serving as an instrument for the safeguarding of the "national interest" in a world of competitive and conflicting as well as cooperative "national interests."

None of these functions could it satisfactorily perform, were the State not endowed with *Danda* (Sanskrit)—shall we say scepter?—the symbol of power as well as the power to punish. Indeed, from this standpoint, the State may be best defined as the embodiment of *Danda,* i.e., of brute force.

Rarely does the State resort to *Danda* in its dealings with in-group members. The judicial machinery providing punishment for the guilty, unto death where necessary, takes care of stresses and strains that are bound to arise in organized relations among human beings. Totalitarian States make freer use of *Danda* in their dealings with citizens than do democratic States; even at that, totalitarian States, too, must, in the final analysis, depend upon methods of persuasion and mild coercion rather than naked brute force.

In its dealings with other entities like unto itself, the State, whether totalitarian or democratic, relies upon diplomacy, a species of duplicity, upon negotiation and treaty, sometimes upon persuasion and arbitration, and judicial interpretation by the World Court, but always upon *Danda,* upon brute force, as the final recourse. The reliance upon brute force by individual States will become outmoded only when mankind evolves a World State with a universally accepted judicial machinery competent to bring about changes in the status quo by peaceful means.

The League of Nations, evolved at end of World War I, made a feeble attempt in this direction. But it failed because it recognized the coexistence of imperiums or empire nations, free nations, and subject nationalities in its membership. The United Nations of the World, evolved at the end of World War II, has an easier task before it because most of the old-style empires have crumbled away; but its task is likely to be equally difficult, and perhaps impossible, because of the rise of the new-style empire, the ideological empire of the Soviet Union. The professed exponents of communist ideology tell us that the free, democratic, capitalist world and the totalitarian, dictatorship communist world cannot coexist indefinitely; that membership in and cooperation with the United Nations is merely a temporary tactical device on the part of the Soviet Union and its satellites. During this century we are witnessing the gradual emergence of two comprehensive sovereignties, totalitarian communist dictatorship sovereignty under the aegis of the Soviet Union on the one hand and democratic sovereignty under the leadership of the United States of America on the other.

The attributes of sovereignty are three: (1) the right to make war and peace at will, (2) the right to maintain armaments at will, (3) the right to be a law unto itself, i.e., recognition of no authority save the authority of "national interest" or the interest of the sovereignty. Thus the State with its sovereignty is indeed a veritable engine of brute force. Deny a State the right to use brute force whenever it chooses, and it ceases to be a sovereign State. The forty-eight States in the Union are not sovereign in the technical sense as is the American State, or the British State, or the Russian State. The U.S.-Canadian Treaty of Arbitration and Conciliation and the Pan-American Union are the only genuine attempts in the direction of "humanizing" the State, involving as they do partial, voluntary renunciation of sovereignty, including use of brute force at will.

Under present conditions, the State by its very nature cannot deny itself the right to use violence when it deems fit and proper. Thus it is crystal-clear that Gandhi, the apostle of non-violence, was not inconsistent in permitting the free India of his vision, the new State of Bharat, the right to maintain an army, "the smallest army imaginable," and to use it in accordance with the logic of the State machinery.

7. GANDHI AND IDEOLOGICAL WARFARE

One of the profoundest of Gandhi's contributions is the distinction he made between the man and the system. The system, whether social, political, economic, religious, or intellectual, has a logic all its own. When an evil system becomes destructive of the well-being of man, it must be "mended or ended," "altered or abolished." But man, the operator of the system, is himself a victim of the system and as such deserves our sympathy and love; he is to be mended, not to be ended; to be redeemed, not to be "liquidated"; to be converted into a co-worker with us. Thus we can have, ought to have, legitimate quarrel with the system of evil—say, the British Empire in India of yesterday or the communist dictatorship in Soviet Russia of today—but we should have no quarrel with or hatred for the people in whose name and by whom the system is operated.

Within this framework, what might we suppose would be Gandhi's response to the conflict between the communist sovereignty and the democratic sovereignty? Five possible ways in which the conflict situation may be resolved suggest themselves: (1) With malice toward none, with charity for all, we must strive, non-violently so far as possible, to mend or to end the communist totalitarian dictatorship system of the Soviet Union; (2) we may submit to the blandishments and exactions of the evil system and earn peace, the peace of the graveyard—an alternative Gandhi would reject wholeheartedly; (3) we must develop creative approaches to the Soviet Union, responses of goodwill to the helpless peoples dominated by the totalitarian dictatorship system the while we work for the mending or ending of that system; (4) we must sacrificially and disinterestedly strengthen the forces of freedom and democracy in the "free" world, i.e., in all the countries still outside the jurisdiction of the Soviet totalitarian dictatorship sovereignty, by fighting the evil conditions: poverty and misery, famine and disease, illiteracy and ill-productivity—conditions which may predispose their victims to listen to the false promises of the communist ideology; (5) we must develop an international authority, armed with power to coerce the recalcitrant members, to bring them in line within the framework of democracy—an authority endowed with a machinery for adjudication of conflicts and for the accomplishment of change in the status quo by peaceful methods. (Coexistence of communism and democracy is ruled out by the communists themselves.)

Within this framework, the mode of operation permissible to American citizens is obvious. We must strive to promote the purposes of alternatives (1), (3), (4), and (5). While attacking the problem on those four fronts, we must strive to build up the armed might of America and of the free world. Preparedness on our part may obviate Soviet aggression; and, in the event of Soviet aggression, it would help us achieve victory for the democratic cause.

8. GANDHI'S QUEST FOR PEACE

As a war resister Gandhi had to be an internationalist. Internationalism, for him, was to be built on the solid foundation of nationalism. "Internationalism is possible only when nationalism becomes a fact, i.e., when peoples belonging to different countries have organized themselves and are able to act as one man." But his nationalism would have no truck with "narrowness, selfishness, exclusiveness." For him patriotism was the same as humanity. "I am patriotic because I am human and humane. . . . My patriotism includes the good of mankind in general." Patriotism, nationalism, is but a prelude to internationalism. "Isolated independence is not the goal of the world States. It is voluntary interdependence. . . . I see nothing grand or impossible about our expressing our readiness for universal interdependence rather than independence." [10]

Gandhi has given a new meaning to nationalism and patriotism. He has also transformed the meaning of the terms war and peace, but he was so deeply engrossed in working out peaceful alternatives to war that he never got around to redefining war and peace. In the light of Gandhi's philosophy, we may attempt a redefinition of war and peace. Both war and peace are dynamic processes, not static events that just happen on a particular date or set of dates. We have war whenever and wherever there are present in the relations among men injustice, oppression, tyranny, exploitation, denial of freedom, denial of the worth of human personality, inflicted by one group upon another, whether nationally or internationally. The search for peace, on the other hand, far from consisting in an absence of war, consists in the constant strivings of men for removal of injustice, oppression, tyranny, exploitation, denial of freedom, denial of the worth of human personality; and peace itself consists in the creation of those conditions and instrumentalities which would, in the words of George Fox, lead mankind "out of the occasions of war" and "out of the earth up to God."

Gandhi's quest for peace resolved itself into constant striv-

ings for the removal of injustice. In other words, Gandhi was concerned with bringing about social change. The strategy and tactics
worked out by the Mahatma have a special message for mankind
in these troublous times.

How do we bring about social change? We bring about social
change in one of three ways: (1) by evolutionary methods including constitutional procedures, advocated by our Republicans,
Democrats, and Socialists; (2) by brute force methods, advocated
by totalitarian ideologists, Fascists, and Communists; (3) by soul
force methods, advocated by Mahatma Gandhi and the historic
peace church groups in Christendom.

It may be instructive to compare and contrast the Marxist-
communist mode of operation with Gandhi's. First, both believe
in the need for change in certain aspects of the social process; but
while the communist would make a complete break with the past,
Gandhi would conserve and preserve as much of the past as would
serve the needs of the better society of tomorrow. Second, the
communist would bring about change by reliance upon violence
and brute force, upon falsehood and deceit, upon "boring from
within" and trampling on the common decencies of mankind;
Gandhi would bring about change by reliance upon non-violence
and soul force, upon truth and love, upon chivalry and appeal to
the best elements of human nature. Third, the communist's goal
is the liquidation of the wrongdoer; Gandhi's goal is the regeneration of the wrongdoer. Fourth, the communist would seize
power, the State machinery, by violence and maintain it by violence—by the imposition of a dictatorship of the proletariat;
Gandhi would think not in terms of power but in terms of service,
not in terms of capturing the State but in terms of transforming
the State into an instrument of general well-being, and he would
maintain the regenerated State not by dictatorship of any segment
of the population but by democratic processes, by the will of the
majority. Fifth, the communist would reduce the individual to an
automaton, a cog in the State machinery; Gandhi would exalt the
worth and dignity of the individual. Sixth, both believe in espousing the cause of the underprivileged and the cause of those to
whom palpable injustice may have been done. The result in both

cases is the same: a swelling of sympathy for the champion of the cause both from the aggrieved and from sections of the general public. The communist would use this device to further his nefarious designs of promoting communism; Gandhi would use this device to purify and regenerate society. Seventh, the communist places blind faith in the possibility of evolving a better world through institutional change; the Mahatma, while working for the mending or ending of certain outmoded institutional patterns, places his main reliance upon sensitized consciences, upon regenerated human beings, for abiding change in society. Eighth, both believe in the all-important role of a specially trained core group in the vanguard of the movement for social change. The communist has his indoctrinated party members operating secretively "in the vanguard of the labor movement," boring from within, giving a lead to innocent workers, gaining the workers' confidence by identifying themselves with the workers' grievances, always working for the overthrow of the State by underhanded methods and by violent methods whenever possible. Gandhi, on the other hand, had his disciplined core of Ashramites, working in the open, identifying themselves with the general welfare, always striving to purify themselves and society.

If the communist today poses a threat to free society, it is because his strategy is well conceived and apparently sound sociologically. A handful of professional revolutionaries, working doggedly twenty-four hours a day while the rest of us are sleeping or sleep-walking, can confound thousands of innocent, ease-loving citizens.

If our free society is to survive and prosper, we shall have to develop a dedicated core of workers, willing to devote themselves to the public good twenty-four hours a day as Gandhi and his noble band did in India. If we were to have a small group of people, religiously motivated, ever on the alert to discover areas of tension and injustice and ready to find creative, non-violent solutions, we would vitalize our democracy and scotch the menace of communism.

The call of *Satyagraha* is imperative and urgent. Cooperate with all, giving the benefit of the doubt to the opposing party; but cooperate only so long as you are not called upon to sacrifice your principles. Non-cooperation is preferable to cooperation if cooperation should involve compromise with principle. Work for peace, never for appeasement, i.e., buying of peace with sacrifice of principles. Integrity of the human soul, not peace, is the highest good. Make concessions on details, never on principles. Work out constructive programs for the nation and for the world. Be ready with your life to defend the precious heritage of freedom and democracy. Practise peace toward men of goodwill and constantly strive to convert men of illwill. Thus shall society be regenerated and man come into his own.

NOTES AND BIBLIOGRAPHY

PREFACE

1. Richard J. Walsh, ed.: *Nehru on Gandhi,* pp. 127–128. New York: The John Day Co., 1948.
2. Mahatma Gandhi: *Sermon on the Sea,* ed. by Haridas T. Muzumdar, p. 96. Chicago: Universal Publishing Co., 1924.
3. See note 1, Chapter One.

CHAPTER ONE

1. Mahatma Gandhi: *Young India 1919–1922,* p. 261. New York: B. W. Huebsch, Inc., 1923. This statement is quoted from Gandhi's famous editorial (*Young India,* August 11, 1920), on "The Doctrine of the Sword" (Ibid., pp. 259–263), reproduced in the present author's *Gandhi the Apostle* (Chicago: Universal Publishing Co., 1923), pp. 188–189, as well as in Jawaharlal Nehru's Autobiography: *Toward Freedom* (New York: The John Day Co., 1941), pp. 81–82.
2. Mahatma Gandhi: *Sermon on the Sea,* ed. by Haridas T. Muzumdar, p. 66. Chicago, now New York: Universal Publishing Co., 1924.

CHAPTER TWO

1. Haridas T. Muzumdar: *Gandhi Versus the Empire,* p. 167. New York: Universal Publishing Co., 1932. The phrase appears in Gandhi's broadcast from London to the American people.

2. *Ibid.*, p. 26. Complete text of the Hindese Declaration of Independence appears on pp. 25–27.
3. Richard J. Walsh, ed.: *Nehru on Gandhi,* p. 26. New York: The John Day Co., 1948.
4. Reginald Heber: *Narrative of a Journey Through the Upper Provinces of India,* p. 286. Philadelphia: Carey, Lea and Carey, 1829.
5. *Ibid.*, p. 287.
6. Joseph J. Doke: *M. K. Gandhi: An Indian Patriot,* p. 84. London: London Indian Chronicle, 1909.
7. John Ruskin: *Unto This Last,* pp. 125–126. New York: John Wiley and Sons, 1885.
8. *Ibid.*, p. 33.
9. *Ibid.*, p. 38.
10. William James: *The Varieties of Religious Experiences* (1902). See Lecture XV on "The Values of Saintliness," wherein for the first time James uses the term, the moral equivalent of war.
11. R. K. Prabhu and U. R. Rao: *The Mind of Mahatma Gandhi,* p. 5. Madras: Oxford University Press, 1945, 2nd ed. 1946.
12. *Ibid.*, p. 13.
13. M. K. Gandhi: *Gandhi's Autobiography: The Story of My Experiments with Truth,* p. 365. Washington: Public Affairs Press, 1948.
14. J. J. Doke: *Op. cit.,* p. 69.
15. C. F. Andrews: *Gandhi at Work,* p. 317. New York: The Macmillan Co., 1931.
16. *Ibid.*, pp. 352–353.
17. *Ibid.*, pp. 389–390.

CHAPTER THREE

1. *Sermon on the Sea,* p. 121.
2. R. K. Prabhu and U. R. Rao: *Op. cit.,* p. 30.
3. *Ibid.*, p. 3.

4. Haridas T. Muzumdar: *Gandhi the Apostle,* pp. 190–191. Chicago, now New York: Universal Publishing Co., 1923.
5. R. K. Prabhu and U. R. Rao: *Op. cit.,* p. 27.
6. *Ibid.,* p. 2.

CHAPTER FOUR

1. Lajpat Rai: *Young India,* p. 115. New York: B. W. Huebsch, Inc., 1917.
2. *Nehru on Gandhi,* p. 1.
3. D. G. Tendulkar, et al.: *Gandhiji,* Bombay: Karnatak Publishing House, 1944. 2nd ed., 1945. Opposite p. 37, photostat copy.
4. Mahatma Gandhi: *Young India 1919–1922,* pp. 608–613. New York: B. W. Huebsch, Inc., 1923.
5. *Ibid.,* pp. 668–675.
6. *Ibid.,* pp. 459–461.
7. *Gandhiji,* p. 38, quoted by Kripalani.
8. *Ibid.,* p. 33.

CHAPTER FIVE

1. *Gandhi the Apostle,* quoted, p. 191. This statement occurs in Gandhi's exposition of the Vow of Non-Thieving, referred to in Chapter Three.
2. M. A. Sohrab, ed.: *The Bible of Mankind,* quoted by Lin Mousheng in his "A Preface to Taoism," p. 286. New York: Universal Publishing Co., 1939.
3. *Ibid.,* pp. 286–287.
4. Mahadev Desai: "How does Mr. Gandhi Live?" p. 3. Srirangam: P. K. Rajagopal, Publisher, 1940.
5. *Gandhi Versus the Empire,* pp. 281–283, condensed.
6. *Sermon on the Sea,* pp. xxi–xxii.
7. *Nehru on Gandhi,* p. ix. (The Foreword in this book originally appeared as a Foreword in *Gandhiji,* 2nd ed., 1945).
8. *Gandhi Versus the Empire,* p. 29. These statements occur in Gandhi's statement at his famous trial on March 18, 1922.

A full account of Gandhi's trial in 1922 appears in my *Gandhi the Apostle,* pp. 145–164.

9. *Gandhiji,* pp. 88–89; quoted by M. R. Masani in his Chapter, "Is Gandhi a Socialist?"
10. *Ibid.,* p. 88.
11. *Gandhiji,* p. 142; Gulzarilal Nanda: "A Charter for Labor."
12. *Ibid.,* p. 142.
13. *Ibid.,* p. 143.
14. *Ibid.,* p. 143.
15. *Ibid.,* pp. 144–145, condensed.
16. *Sermon on the Sea,* p. 92.
17. *Gandhi Versus the Empire,* pp. 325–326. Also reproduced in my book, *The United Nations of the World,* p. 141; New York: Universal Publishing Co., 1942; 2nd ed., 1944.
18. *Gandhiji,* p. 84, quoted by M. R. Masani.
19. *Harijan, Ahmedabad,* May 10, 1952.

CHAPTER SIX

1. Some Aspects of Gandhi's pedagogy were brought to the attention of American educators by me for the first time in 1935. The first two illustrations, "Gandhi and the English Children" and "Gandhi and Montessori," originally appeared in my book *Gandhi Versus the Empire* (1932), pp. 157–158. Sections of this chapter appeared in *School and Society,* and in *Unity* (Chicago, Ill.).
2. *School and Society,* Lancaster, Pa., Vol. 42, Sept. 28, 1935, pp. 436–438.
3. The remainder of this section and the following one appeared in a slightly different form in *Unity,* Chicago, Vol. CXVIII, No. 3, October 5, 1936.
4. Mahatma Gandhi: *Sermon on the Sea,* ed. by Haridas T. Muzumdar, p. 104. Chicago, now New York: Universal Publishing Co., 1924.
5. *Ibid.,* pp. 43 ff.
6. *Ibid.,* pp. 72–73.
7. *Ibid.,* pp. xxi–xxii, adapted.

8. *Ibid.*, pp. 101–102.
9. *Ibid.*, pp. 102–103.
10. *Ibid.*, p. 104.
11. Mahatma Gandhi: *The Indian Opinion*, Phoenix, Natal, South Africa, Vol. XXXV, No. 25, June 18, 1937; quoted on the cover.
12. Carleton Washburne: *Remakers of Mankind*, pp. 104–105. New York: The John Day Co., 1932.
13. C. F. Andrews: *Mahatma Gandhi's Ideas*, p. 200. New York: The Macmillan Co., 1930.
14. *Ibid.*, p. 101.
15. This section originally appeared in a slightly different form in *The Social Frontier*, December, 1938 (New York, Vol. V, No. 40, pp. 77–81).
16. *Harijan*, Poona, October 2, 1937.

CHAPTER SEVEN

1. *Gandhiji*, p. xi.
2. *Gandhi the Apostle*, p. 192.
3. *Ibid.*, p. 196.
4. *Ibid.*, pp. 198–199.
5. *The World Tomorrow*, New York, Vol. 11, No. 11, November, 1928, p. 447.
6. *Young India 1919–1922*, pp. 658–662.
7. M. K. Gandhi: *Speeches and Writings*, pp. 201–202. Madras: G. A. Natesan and Co., 1919. See, also, my *Gandhi the Apostle*, p. 119.
8. *Young India, 1919–1922*, pp. 660.
9. *Ibid.*, p. 260.
10. *Gandhiji*, pp. 313–314; abstracted from a compilation of Gandhi's statements on nationalism and internationalism. My thanks go to the anonymous compiler.

CHRONOLOGY

1869   —Born October 2 at Porbandar in Kathiawad, Gujarat.
1884   —Experiments in meat-eating; became an agnostic.
1888–1891—Landed in England in September, 1888. Carried on experiments to make of himself an English gentleman. Enrolled as a law student at the Inner Temple. Became acquainted with the Sermon on the Mount and with the Bhagavad Gita. Called to the bar June 10, 1891; enrolled in the High Court the next day and sailed for home on June 12, 1891.
1891–1893—Indifferent attempts at legal practice in India.
1893–1914—Went to South Africa, end of May, 1893, as legal retainer for a Muslim Hindese firm. Suffered personal humiliations at the hands of European colonists who treated with contempt Asians as well as Africans. Enrolled as a barrister in the High Courts of Natal and the Transvaal over the opposition of European lawyers. Established Phoenix Ashram in 1904 and the Tolstoy Farm Ashram in 1910. Led the Great March from Natal into the Transvaal October 30, 1913; arrested in South Africa for the last time November 9, 1913; sentenced to rigorous imprisonment, November 11, 1913; released December 18, 1913; arrived at final settlement with General Smuts in 1914. Sailed for London en route to India. Arrived in England August 6, 1914, two days after World War I began. Organized an Ambulance Corps of Hindese students in London.

Because of ill-health, he left England in December, 1914.

1915   —Landed in Bombay on the 9th of January.

1916   —Established the Satyagraha Ashram.

1917   —Led the no-tax campaign in Kheda District.

1918   —Recruited men for the British armed forces when the Allied side was threatened gravely.

1919   —Led the Passive Resistance campaign against the Rowlatt Act.

1920   —Launched the Non-Violent Non-Cooperation Movement for the attainment of Swaraj by India.

1922   —Arrested on March 12, 1922. Tried on March 18 and sentenced to six years' imprisonment.

1924   —Released from prison after an operation for appendicitis by an English surgeon.

1930   —During his period of retirement from politics (1924–1929) he organized the All-India Spinners' Association with branches all over India. In 1929, called back to assume leadership of the Congress. The Declaration of Independence, prepared by him, was proclaimed and read all over India on January 26, 1930. On March 12 he began the March to the Sea with 78 volunteers including the present author. Reached Dandi on April 5. After a purificatory bath in the refreshing waters of the ocean, Gandhi and his volunteers broke the salt law on April 6, and thus initiated nationwide civil disobedience. May 5 Gandhi was arrested.

1931   —Gandhi released January 26. Gandhi-Irwin Pact signed on March 4. The Mahatma went to London to attend the Second Round Table Conference, September 12 to December 5. Visited Romain Rolland in Switzerland December 6–11. Landed in Bombay December 28.

1932   —Arrested January 4 and detained in Yeravada Prison. September 20, started his "fast unto death" against Prime Minister MacDonald's Communal

Award. September 24 the Yeravada Pact was signed, in presence of fasting Gandhi, by high-caste and low-caste Hindus. The terms of this Pact, supplanting the MacDonald award, were accepted by the British government on September 26, and Gandhi broke his fast amidst world-wide rejoicing.

1933 —February, from behind prison bars, Gandhi founded the Harijan Sevak Sangh—the Association of Servants of Untouchables—and the *Harijan* weekly paper. Released on May 8, the day he started his twenty-one-day purificatory fast in behalf of the Harijans.

1934–1940—Formally retired from Congress, but "reigned" as the "Paramount Power" both inside the Congress and outside during the rest of his life, which opened a new chapter in his activities—crusade against untouchability, promotion of handicrafts including spinning and weaving, organization of village rehabilitation work, launching of a basic education movement. The Sevagram Ashram "grew up" during this period.

1940 —Launched limited individual civil disobedience— not a mass movement—in protest against India's enforced participation in World War II.

1942 —Sir Stafford Cripps arrived at Karchi, March 12, reached Delhi on the 23rd, and had an interview with Gandhi on the 27th. Cripps Mission failed to rally Hindese behind war effort, but it laid groundwork for the later emergence of Pakistan. August 8, at Gandhi's behest, the All-India Congress Committee, meeting in Bombay, passed the "Quit India" resolution. The British Raj accepted the challenge, imprisoned Gandhi in the Aga Khan Palace, Poona, and rounded up thousands of Congress leaders throughout the country. August 15, Mahadev Desai, Gandhi's secretary and fellow prisoner, died.

1944 —February 22, Mrs. Gandhi died in the Aga Khan

Palace. May 6 Gandhi was released from Prison—
the Aga Khan Palace—unconditionally in view of
his ill-health. Since release from prison, Gandhi devoted himself to "the constructive program" for
achieving India's freedom—a dream that was realized three years later.

1947 —August 15, British India was divided into two self-
governing Dominions by the British Raj—the Dominion of India and the Dominion of Pakistan. The
division of India engendered bitterness between
Hindus and Muslims. Enforced mass migrations of
Muslims into Pakistan and of non-Muslims into
India fanned the flames of bitterness. Gandhi began
to plead for equal rights and protection for the
Muslim minority—40 millions—left in India. The
militant Hindu wing would drive all Muslims into
Pakistan, now that India was divided.

1948 —While he was engaged in the service of his dearly
beloved Motherland, in reconciling Hindus and
Muslims, Gandhi was struck by an assassin's bullet
(January 30) as he was on his way to the evening
prayer-meeting. Hands prayerfully folded about his
forehead, both as an act of prayer, the last for him,
and as a gesture of forgiveness to the assassin,
Gandhi passed out of this life with the words:
Rāma, Rāma—Oh Lord! Oh Lord!

1950 —January 26, India proclaimed herself a Republic,
the new State of Bharat, with due reverence for
the martyred Mahatma.

INDEX

Ahimsa, 23, 41, 86 ff., 98 ff.
Ahmedabad Textile Labor Association, 64–66
All-India National Congress, 46
America, 19, 68, 69, 109, 110
Amritsar, 55
Appraisals, 96, 97
Arnold, Sir Edwin, 10
Arrests, 7, 29
Ashram, 14, 23 ff., 31, 47, 59
Asoka, 99

Bengal, India, 45, 47, 55
Bhagavad Gita, the, 3, 9, 10, 11, 19, 57
Bhavé, Vinoba, 72–74
British Empire, loyalty to, 104
British Imperialism, 5, 6, 12–15
Brute Force, 2, 38, 39, 69, 108, 109
Buddha, 23, 34, 36, 75

Capital, Karl Marx's, 58
Carpenter, Edward, 80
Children, Gandhi and, 77, 78
Clothes, crusade for burning of foreign, 48, 50, 51
Communal Award, MacDonald's, 54
Communism, 66 ff., 98, 108 ff.
C.I.O., the, 32
Concern for others, 33, 34, 98
Conscience, 3 ff., 85, 100, 104

Crown of Wild Olive, The, Ruskin's, 20

Dandi, ix, 2, 7, 31
Darwin, Charles, 38, 39
Declaration of Independence, Indian, 17
Democracy, 41, 42, 67, 101, 105 ff.
Desai, Mahadev, 54, 57
Dharna, 17, 18
"Doctrine of the Sword, The," 106
Doke, Rev. and Mrs. Joseph J., 14
Douglas, Paul H., 99

Economics, Gandhi's, 57–74
Education, 9–11, 75–94
Einstein, Albert, 96
England, 10–13
Essay on Civil Disobedience, Thoreau's, 19
Experimentation, 7–11, 18, 30, 33, 47

Fair Employment Practices Commission, 32
Family, 6–10
Fasts, 54, 64
Fox, George, 37, 111
Freedom, 83, 84

Gandhi Day, at Shantiniketan, 55
Gandhi, Manilal, 24

Gayatri, 81
Great March, 27–29
Guide to Health, Gandhi's, 26
Gujarat National University, 87

Hamilton, Sir Daniel, 60
Harijan, 57
Harijans, 78, 87, 88
Heber, Bishop Reginald, 17, 18
Hind Swaraj, Gandhi's, 30
Hindese, the, 16, 17, 27, 98
Hinduism, 7, 8, 87
Hobbes, Thomas, 38, 39
Hodgend, J. Z., 96
Hoover, Herbert, 99
Husain, Dr. Zakir, 90, 94
Huxley, Professor, 82, 83
Hyderabad State, 72, 73

India, Free, 70 ff.
Indian Opinion, 24, 25
Industrialism, 12, 13, 61–63
Internationalism, 55, 108, 110

Jallianwalla Bagh massacre, 55
James, William, 16, 20, 21, 34
Jesus, 34, 36, 75, 78, 89

Kallenbach, Hermann, 14, 25
Kidd, Benjamin, 38
*Kingdom of God Is Within You,
The,* Tolstoy's, 19
Kripalani, K. R., quoted, 56
Kropotkin, Peter, 38

Labor movement in India, 63 ff.
Land-Gifts Movement, 72–74
Laotze, 58, 75
Leadership, 30–35, 75
League of Nations, 108

Mahabharata, the, quotation from, 3, 104
Malthus, Thomas Robert, 38, 39

March to the Sea, 31, 32
Marx, Karl, 58, 66 ff.
Marxism, 39, 60, 61, 66–71
Masani, M. R., 67
Montessori, Mme., M. 75 ff.
Morris, William, 12
Meat-eating, 8, 10
Modern Review, The, Calcutta, 48, 49
Moral Equivalent of War, 16 ff.
Mott, Dr. John R., 59
Mukta-Dhara (The Waterfall), Tagore's, 53
Murray, Gilbert, 97

Namaz, 81
Nanda, Mr., quoted, 64
Nationalism, in India, 6, 15, 30
Nature cure, 26
Nehru, Pandit Jawaharlal, 17, 60
quoted, 46–47, 98
Newcastle, 27
Non-violent non-cooperation movement, 41 ff.
Non-violent resistance, 2, 14, 15, 16 ff., 30 ff., 64, 86, 87, 100 ff.

One World, 4, 5

Pacifism, 101, 102, 106 ff.
Pan-American Union, the, 109
Peace, quest for, 111–114
Pedagogy, Gandhi's, 75 ff.
Penn, William, 99
Pestalozzi, 75, 94
Phoenix, South Africa, 24, 25, 27, 47, 55, 76, 87
Plato, 57, 75, 106
Polak, Mr. and Mrs. H. S. L., 14
Porbandar, 17
Preparedness, 110

Quakers, 2, 19, 99, 100

Racialism, 12–15
Reforms espoused by Gandhi, 34
Religion, 6 ff., 87, 98
Ruskin, John, 12, 20, 60
Russia, 67 ff., 108, 109

Sabarmati, 23, 31
Sarvodaya movement, 73, 74
Satyagraha, 21, 23, 41, 42, 53, 101, 113
Satyagraha Ashram, 23, 87 ff.; eightfold vow, 31, 33, 87
Self-inflicted suffering, 40–42
Sermon on the Mount, 11, 14, 18
Sevagram Ashram, 59
Shantiniketan, 47, 54, 55
Smuts, General, 15, 29
Socialism, 57, 67 ff.
Song Celestial, The, 10
Soul Force, 2, 15, 18, 22, 30 ff.
South Africa, 12–14; Gandhi's march, 27–29
Soviet Union, *see* Russia
Spinning wheel, the, 13, 48, 50
Swadeshi, 31, 33, 51, 87

Tagore, Rabindranath, 45–56, 97
Thoreau, Henry David, 13, 14, 19

Tolstoy, Leo, 13, 14, 16, 19
Tolstoy Farm, 25, 26
Translations, 57
Truth, 7, 22, 41, 87

United Nations of the World, 108
U. S.-Canadian Treaty of Arbitration and Conciliation, 109
Universals, 1–4
Unto This Last, Ruskin's, 20, 24, 57
Untouchability, 76 ff.

Vaihinger, 39
Village Industries and Reconstruction Association, 63

Wardha Scheme of Education, 90–95
Warfare, 101 ff.
Washburne, Dr. Carleton, 85, 86
Waterfall, The, Tagore's, 53
West, Mr. and Mrs. A. H., 14

Yeravada Prison, 54
Young India, xi, 48, 49, 52